OLD TESTAMENT
WISDOM

The Storyteller's Companion to the Bible ™

Michael E. Williams, editor

VOLUME FIVE

OLD TESTAMENT WISDOM

Abingdon Press
Nashville

OLD TESTAMENT WISDOM

Library of Congress Cataloging-in-Publication Data
(Revised for vol. 5)

The Storyteller's companion to the Bible.
  Includes indexes.
  Contents: v. 1. Genesis—v. 2. Exodus-Joshua—[etc.]—v. 5. Old Testament wisdom.

  1. Bible—Paraphrases, English. 2. Bible—Criticism, interpretation, etc. I. Williams,
Michael E. (Michael Edward), 1950-
BS550.2.S764   1991   220.9'505   90-26289
ISBN 0-687-39670-0 (v. 1 : alk. paper)
ISBN 0-687-39671-9 (v. 2 : alk. paper)
ISBN 0-687-39672-7 (v. 3 : alk. paper)
ISBN 0-687-39674-3 (v. 4 : alk. paper)
ISBN 0-687-39675-1 (v. 5 : alk. paper)

98 99 00 01 02 03 — 10 9 8 7 6 5 4 3 2

MANUFACTURED IN THE UNITED STATES OF AMERICA

For
Margaret
Sarah
and
Elizabeth

(M.E.W.)

For
Ron

(S.H.)

Contributors

Sharon Hels is the editor of *Quarterly Review: A Journal of Theological Resources for Ministry* and the Director in the Office of Interpretation at The United Methodist Board of Higher Education and Ministry. She has taught Old Testament at Scarritt Graduate School and at the School of Theology at the University of the South in Sewanee, Tennessee.

Peninnah Schram is Associate Professor of Speech and Drama at Stern College of Yeshiva University. As a storyteller, she travels across the United States and other countries presenting storytelling workshops and performances of stories from various Jewish sources and folktales from around the world. She is the Founding Director of The Jewish Storytelling Center and Coordinator of The Jewish Storytelling Network.

Donald Davis, a United Methodist pastor, is a professional storyteller who travels the world telling stories and teaching others. Numerous books and tapes contain his stories, including *Listening for the Crack of Dawn, Barking at a Fox-Fur Coat, Jack Always Seeks His Fortune,* and *Telling Your Own Stories.*

Michael E. Williams is one of the pastors at Belle Meade United Methodist Church in Nashville, Tennessee. He earned his Ph.D. in oral interpretation from Northwestern University and previously directed the Office of Preaching for The United Methodist Church.

Contents

A Storyteller's Companion

Michael E. Williams

This volume, like the previous four in the Storyteller's Companion to the Bible Series, is for anyone interested in telling Bible stories. But this volume is significantly different from its predecessors in that, with the exception of the book of Job, it does not begin with stories from the Bible. Rather, here we begin with the teachings and sayings of the wisdom tradition of the Hebrew Bible. Pastors who encounter readings in the lectionary from the wisdom tradition or who choose to preach on wisdom texts will find this book particularly helpful as they prepare to put the flesh and blood of a sermon on the skeleton provided by a proverb. If preaching is to help the listener to participate in the world of the Scriptures, then telling stories that make the teachings of the thinkers of our faith tradition come alive is imperative.

In addition, leaders of Bible studies may be called upon to "explain" the meaning of a wisdom saying. What better way to answer a call for explanation than the ways the ancient rabbis and sages did, by telling a story? The first four volumes have been used for personal Bible study by many individuals looking for alternate resources for enriching their knowledge of Scripture. It may also be that parents or grandparents will want to tell stories that flesh out some bit of traditional wisdom as they act as the first and perhaps most significant teachers in their families.

We live in what some call the information age, and we truly have more facts about a greater variety of subjects at our fingertips than during any previous time in history. To gather many bits of information without seeing any pattern in which they have meaning for us is a very trivial pursuit, as the name of the game suggests. We might say that to have knowledge rather than just an assortment of facts means that we know the *why* behind the *what*. This is often provided by the system of shared values within a society. We might call this sort of knowledge conventional wisdom.

When I was a graduate student at Northwestern University, I had the good fortune to study with Edward T. Hall, a noted anthropologist and professor. In our very first session of a class called "Culture as Communication," he gave us a copy of the custom law of Zia Pueblo. The document he passed among the class members was an attempt by the council of Zia Pueblo to explain their common law to Anglo attorneys. The first thing I noticed about the document was that it was two and one-half legal pages long. Can you imagine a city council, much less a state or nation, distilling its entire body of laws into such a brief space? Yet here it was, the common law of Zia Pueblo.

As I worked with the document more, I noticed that, though it was written as prose in paragraphs, some of its language had the heightened and repetitive qualities of poetry. So I set part of the legal document into poetic lines. While it did not rhyme as some poetry in English does, it did exhibit a structure of parallel lines similar to Hebrew poetry. Obviously I am not arguing for a historical relationship here but to note the similarities between two forms of poetic speech that are both oral in their origins.

What Hall had given us was just the distilled remains of the conventional wisdom of life together at Zia. Each line reminded the listeners of stories of those who had chosen to follow or break the tradition. The stories were not repeated in the document because everybody knew such stories and that these narratives were the why behind the conventional duties (whats) written in the law. Remember, the law was written down only for the benefit of those outside the culture, because those within already knew.

In some sense, proverbial wisdom is like the written laws of Zia Pueblo. They represent the conventional wisdom of their time. In addition, behind every proverb is a story that offers the lived experience of the wisdom that the saying points to. Hebrew wisdom is earthy, incarnated, lived wisdom even when it appears in its most abstract clothing. Our task in this volume is to discover those stories that retell the saying in its larger incarnation, as it is lived out in experience or imagination.

The Stories

While we attempt in this volume to be comprehensive in our approach to the wisdom literature of the Hebrew Bible and the Apocrypha, we obviously could not include them all. We have included the texts that appear in *The Revised Common Lectionary,* 1992 (the most inclusive so far). We have gone far beyond the scope of these lectionaries to include stories that make a significant contribution to the biblical wisdom tradition as a whole.

If you do not find one of your favorite passages in this collection, there is no need to despair. Much of the information you will learn from the comments on the stories that are included can be transferred to other texts. This will allow you to use your creativity more fully.

The translation from which the printed texts in this companion are taken is *The Revised English Bible.* You may wish to compare the readings here with your favorite translation or several others. It enriches the telling of biblical stories, especially for those who do not read the original language, to work from various translations.

Comments on the Stories

Sharon Hels holds a Ph.D. in Hebrew Bible from Vanderbilt University and presently serves as editor of *Quarterly Review*. Her comments on the wisdom texts begin the process of putting a face on the teachers whose textbooks are collected there. Based on historical evidence and scholarly research, the persona of each sage is reconstructed. This task might be compared to painting a portrait of a historical figure based entirely on written descriptions—much must be left to the informed imagination. Hels' imagination is well informed and sensitive to the narrative possibilities of each text. The unearthing of stories that embody these lessons gets a strong start from her excellent commentaries.

The specific contribution you will make to the preparation for telling one of these stories is knowing your audience. You can take the information Sharon Hels offers and shape a telling of the story that will be appropriate to the ages and life experiences of your listeners. Only you can know where in the lives of those in your congregation, class, or family a story will strike a chord, turn on a light, or heal a hurt. For more information on how to prepare a story for a specific group of listeners, refer to "Learning to Tell Bible Stories: A Self-directed Workshop" on pp. 21-22.

Retelling the Stories

As a storyteller, you will contribute something of your own personality and understanding of the Bible and your listeners to the telling of a story based on a biblical text. There is no one right way to accomplish this. While this companion includes a sample retelling of each story, these are only examples of one way a story may be told. You may choose to tell it very differently.

The retellings are intended to free your imagination for telling and not to limit you to any one form. Some retellings here are fairly straightforward recountings of a text. Others choose a character or characters from whose point of view to tell the story. Some retellings place the story in a modern world. We hope they will offer you a sample of the vast number of ways Bible stories can come to life in storytelling.

The goal of each retelling is to help our listeners to hear the wisdom of the lesson as if for the first time and to see the world of the lesson as something new and fresh. We are grateful for the imaginations of the storytellers who provided the retellings for this volume:

Peninnah Schram is associate professor of speech and drama at Stern College of Yeshiva University. A professional storyteller, she founded and directs the Jewish Storytelling Center of New York and the National Jewish Storytelling Network. Among her many books, records, and tapes are *Jewish Stories*

One Generation Tells Another and *Tales of Elijah the Prophet.* Peninnah brings a particular authenticity to the Jewish wisdom tradition, since she grew up surrounded by its saying and stories.

Donald Davis, a United Methodist pastor for over twenty years, is now a professional storyteller who travels the world telling stories and teaching others to reclaim and retell their own stories. Always a favorite teller at the National Storytelling Festival, Donald was raised in a family storytelling tradition in Haywood County, North Carolina. These roots prepared him for the numerous tapes and books that contain his stories. These include *Listening for the Crack of Dawn, Barking at a Fox-Fur Coat, Jack Always Seeks His Fortune,* and most recently *Telling Your Own Stories.* Donald's retellings call forth our own wisdom stories, the ones we disregard or simply do not see most of the time.

Peninnah retells the stories based on texts from Proverbs and Ecclesiastes. Donald's retellings emerge from lessons from the Wisdom of Solomon, and I retell the texts from Job and those from Ecclesiasticus.

Midrashim

If you ask a rabbi a question, you are likely to get a story for an answer. This reflects a wisdom that knows truth to be irreducible to a one-two-three answer. Truth is embodied in events as they happen and in persons as they relate to each other and to God. This kind of truth is best experienced in stories and concrete images. Perhaps no book is a better example of this storied truth telling than the Bible.

The most unique contribution this companion makes to the art of biblical storytelling is to include the stories and sayings of the ancient rabbis related to the wisdom sayings and stories. These are midrashim (the singular is midrash), from a Hebrew word that means "to go in search of." When the rabbis went in search of the relevance of these already "old, old stories" for their time, they returned with questions. Those questions generated stories that stand alongside the Scripture passages and interpret them in ways that children and adults alike can understand.

The midrashim included here came from several sources, and I have retold and adapted them for inclusion here. These midrashim appear in boxed text in the retelling of each story, placed near the part of the story to which they most closely relate. As you retell the story, you may wish to include one or more of the midrashim at these points in the story or at other appropriate places. For more information, refer to "What Are Midrashim, and What Are They Doing Here?" on pages 18-20.

You will probably not want to read this companion from front to back as you would most books. It is not designed to be read that way. One way to make effective use of it would be first to read Sharon Hels' introduction to her comments on the stories and the introduction to midrash. Then choose a story that you wish to tell. This may be a story from an upcoming Sunday of the lectionary or the church school curriculum, or it may simply be a story that captures your interest. Once you have chosen the story, work through the short workshop on storytelling, using the story you chose as your content.

Use the retelling provided with the story as a guide, but do not feel obligated to simply repeat it. Tell the story for your hearers in your own way. You may choose to include the midrashim with your retelling, or you may tell them afterward. In any case, you are about to take part in one of the most ancient experiences people do in community: offering the gift of God's story so that it touches our story today.

Introduction to Wisdom Literature

Sharon Hels

For most of us, the word *wisdom* is associated with timeless truths and the deep-seated currents of human existence. We think of stories, on the other hand, as entertaining, their plots driven by the waves of everyday emotions and occurrences. Wisdom is dignified and grand; stories are engaging and commonplace. There are exceptions, of course: stories with a strong moral lesson, such as Aesop's fables or some of the folktales collected by the Grimm brothers or Hans Christian Andersen. Likewise, philosophers and poets may use stories to illustrate their ideas. But the storyteller who wishes to express something of the depth and meaning of human existence—wisdom's content—has no ready-made stock of stories to turn to. Instead, he or she must listen carefully for the wisdom to be found in familiar stories, or construct new ones based on wisdom's time-honored forms: the proverb, the riddle, and the analogy.

In ancient Israel, too, wisdom—or *hokmah,* to use the Hebrew term—was not essentially story-based. The wisdom literature, including the books of Proverbs, Job, Ecclesiastes, Sirach, and the Wisdom of Solomon, does not contain individual stories, or narratives, like the stories about the mothers and fathers of Israel in Genesis or those about national leaders in the books of Samuel and Kings. The sole exception to this is the book of Job, which is based on a legend about an exemplary man who suffers terrible afflictions but remains faithful. Israelite wisdom appears to be deliberately nonhistorical. It does not refer to Israel's epic story of liberation from slavery in Egypt and pilgrimage to the Promised Land. King Solomon, who is lavishly credited with the rise of wisdom in Israel during his own lifetime (c.950 B.C.E., see 1 Kings 3–4) is cited as the author of Ecclesiastes and the Wisdom of Solomon. Both books were actually composed centuries after his death. But the most troublesome thing, perhaps, is that there are no stories about the wise men and women of Israel themselves. In fact, in the period in which Israel's classic literature was being collected and compiled, what we think of as the biblical period, neither they nor their schools make any direct appearance. We know that they existed, but we know it only from their proverbs.

How can biblical wisdom literature as a whole be so heavily dependent on one short form of expression? Scholars have pointed out that Israel's understanding of the proverb, or *mashal,* was not restricted to what we consider to be a proverb today. Susan Niditch's study of ethnic literary forms in the Hebrew Bible (*Folklore in the Hebrew Bible* [Philadelphia: Fortress, 1993]) has emphasized this point. In Israel, the *mashal* was not simply a maxim or a saying, such as "A stitch in time saves nine" or "Early to bed, early to rise . . ." although it often appears in that guise. The root meaning of *mashal* has to do with comparisons, analogies, or metaphors. Although it is usually translated into the English word *proverb,* the term *mashal* is applied throughout the Hebrew Bible to literary forms as diverse as songs, poetry, instruction, and even prophetic oracles. In some cases, it was even used to describe people who are said to be a "byword" (see Job 17:6; Ps. 69:11; Jer. 24:9).

We see the greatest concentration of proverbial wisdom in the book of Proverbs, but it is not restricted to that book. Popular sayings can be found in biblical narrative and the prophets (for example, see 1 Sam. 10:11-12; Ezek. 18:2). Proverbs contains both folk wisdom, coming from daily life in Israelite clans, and a more studious form of expression that was carefully crafted by Israel's wise men and women. The editor of Ecclesiastes described this process when he paid tribute to the book's author: "He chose his words to give plea-sure, but what he wrote was straight truth" (Eccles. 12:10). Behind this simple term, therefore, is a reality more complex than we have realized. Beginning with the simple impulse to formulate apt and enlightening comparisons, the *mashal* blossoms into a multitude of forms and topics, all of which are, in a sense, deemed to be "wisdom."

In literary terms, "story" and "proverb" appear to be different because one has a plot and characters, and the other brings two unlike things together to make a comparison between them. But if we search for the roots of these forms in Israelite life through the centuries, we eventually find more similarities than differences. Both owe their existence to the Israelites' need and gift for self-expression in daily life, particularly as it was organized into the spheres of home life, government, marketplace, school, and practice of religion. Both are highly sophisticated, despite their apparent simplicity. Proverbs were handed down from generation to generation by word of mouth, just as Israel's histori-cal memories were handed down. They were shaped by scholars and editors, just as her stories were blended and arranged into sequence. And they were used, like Israel's historical recollections, to make sense of the present, to orga-nize it and give it meaning.

These points can be amplified in three areas that suggest the richness of the links between wisdom and narrative in ancient Israel and may help the story-teller make connections between the wisdom literature and more familiar nar-rative sections of the Bible.

1. Like Israel's historical reminiscences—the stories of Abraham, Isaac, and Jacob; of Moses, Deborah, Ahab, and the rest—Israelite proverbs are indelibly

Israelite. They belong to Israel in the sense that they have been passed down from generation to generation as the special possession of a single people. Wisdom in the form of a *mashal* is first of all received knowledge, what our fathers and mothers taught us, and what we know to be true. In the psalms, the received wisdom includes Israel's story of salvation by God:

> My people, mark my teaching [Torah],
> listen to the words I am about to speak.
> I shall tell you a meaningful story [*mashal*];
> I shall expound the riddle of things past,
> things that we have heard and know,
> things our forefathers have recounted to us.
> They were not hidden from their descendants,
> who will repeat them to the next generation:
> the praiseworthy acts of the LORD
> and the wonders he has done. (Ps. 78:1-4)

Tradition, as Jaroslav Pelikan has written, is the living faith of the dead. If they are to survive, proverbs and stories require that individual people cultivate the ability to remember them and the motivation to pass them on. The effect of this activity is to build a community of people who know who they are and where they stand in the world.

2. The *mashal* is not only specific to one culture, in this case Israel and early Judaism, but it also tells us something about what is universally human. This point is made by scholars who study the relationship between Israelite wisdom and that of the surrounding cultures in the ancient Near East (for more on this, see James L. Crenshaw, *Old Testament Wisdom: An Introductiom* [Atlanta: John Knox, 1981]). In ancient times, wisdom was able to cross ethnic boundaries with surprising ease. For example, both Israelites and Egyptians preserved portions of the *Instruction of Amenenopet,* some of which will be found in our readings. The quality of wisdom that permitted such an exchange is its underlying affirmation of what is real and valuable to human beings living in community. Certain themes recur in proverbial literature, in the same way that themes and patterns recur in stories. These include issues such as the relationships between old and young, between men and women, rich and poor, what constitutes proper piety and social behavior, the nature of virtue, honor, honesty, evildoing, and the like. Stories and proverbs that crossed ethnic barriers can also cross the barriers of time. In addition to the religious authority of our texts, much of the pleasure we receive from them comes from their vital, essentially human quality, for in these proverbs we recognize ourselves and our own concerns. Making the human connection through wisdom texts may be enough to evoke powerful stories of our own.

3. Like stories, proverbs require listener participation. The proverb is com-

pact and subtle; it leaves things out; it may not mean what it seems to at first. Niditch writes that proverbs are intentionally oblique in order to invite the hearer to incorporate his or her own powers of discernment, which may result in more than one interpretation of what is heard. The teller of proverbs, like the storyteller, is joined with the listener in a kind of hidden pact: The teller must discern the proper circumstance in which to relate the *mashal,* and the hearer must recognize this and volunteer his or her own experience as a way to receive and profit from the *mashal.* The same process could be carried out with a story, or the process could begin with a *mashal* and end with a story and vice versa. The *mashal* crossed with a story becomes a parable, used frequently for teaching by rabbis in post-biblical times, including Hillel, Gamaliel, and the writers of the Talmud. For Christians, the parables of Christ are not only meant as illustrations in teaching, but as transformative stories in themselves as well. Structurally, they are simple analogies ("The kingdom of heaven is like . . . "). Yet their goal is not only to teach something about the reign of God but to evoke its reality in the listeners.

In sum, the wisdom literature awaits the storyteller's touch. One does not need to force a narrative grid on these texts. Given enough time and reflection, our encounter with this unusual biblical material may produce something new—tales of wisdom to be passed down in their turn.

What Are Midrashim, and What Are They Doing Here?

Michael E. Williams

Midrash (the plural in Hebrew is *midrashim)* comes from a Hebrew word meaning "to go in search of" or "to inquire." So midrashim resulted when the ancient rabbis went in search of (inquired into) the meaning of the Scriptures for their lives. Midrash is also the name for the process of inquiring into the Scriptures for their meaning.

We might say that midrash is both our encounter with the biblical stories as we seek their meaning for our lives and times and the stories that emerge to express that meaning. Often midrashim do take the form of stories or pieces of stories (at least the ones we will focus on here do). These stories seek to answer questions about and to fill gaps in the biblical stories.

The midrashim drawn from for this volume come from the period 400–1200 C.E. (what is sometimes called A.D.). They were told, in part, to make the stories of women relevant to a Jewish community that had no homeland, could not hold citizenship in other countries, and experienced hostility and persecution from the outside, including from Christian authorities. Most of these midrashim originated in sermons preached in synagogues, based on the prescribed weekly readings from the Torah (the first five books of the Bible). Others emerged from the popular folk traditions of the Jewish communities. Though they were collected and written during that six-hundred period, there is no way of knowing how long the midrashim had been circulating by word of mouth before someone wrote them down. Some are attributed to rabbis living at the time of Jesus. In fact, certain scholars find evidence that this way of interpreting the Bible has its roots intertwined with the texts of the biblical stories themselves.

I see three basic functions for the midrashim I have selected to be included in this book. The first might be called "filling the gaps." These stories and story fragments answer questions about the biblical stories that the Scripture leaves unanswered. When the rabbis answered such questions, they revealed both their fertile imaginations and their own understanding of God and human beings. Sunday school teachers and college professors will also have encountered these imaginative questions.

The second function of midrash is to draw an analogy. These stories begin with "This may be compared to. . . . " Then the rabbi would tell a contemporary story that exhibited a situation and characters like the biblical story under consideration. You may notice that these stories sometimes bear a resemblance to the parables of Jesus and the *mashal* (parable) form of Jewish teaching.

The third function is to describe an encounter. In these stories someone comes to a rabbi with a question, and the rabbi's response interprets both the biblical story and the situation from which the question emerged.

Why did I choose a predominantly Jewish form of interpretation in this book? First, Christians have too often ignored this ancient and time-honored way to interpret the Bible. Given our Jewish roots and Jesus' heritage, midrash is at least as directly related to our tradition as the Greco-Roman philosophy on which we have depended so heavily for ordering our questions and structuring our theological doctrines.

Second, midrashim provide us with a way of interpreting the Bible that involves the imagination and speaks to our experience. It is also, according to certain scholars, the way the Bible interprets itself.

Third, midrashim provide a model for a community-based, inclusive (even children can imaginatively participate in stories), nonprofessional (you don't have to be a trained theologian) way of interpreting the Bible for our times. In short, we can learn the stories the rabbis told about the scriptures to interpret them for their time. In addition, we can follow the example of the rabbis and learn to tell stories about Bible stories that interpret them for our time.

In addition to these reasons I have a personal appreciation for the Jewish storytelling tradition. My intellectual and artistic interests in Jewish narrative range from the Torah to midrash to hasidic stories to modern writers like Isaac Bashevis Singer and Elie Wiesel.

This is just the first step to reclaiming midrashim for modern tellers of Bible stories, but it is a step. If you want to learn more about midrashim related to the wisdom tradition, you may wish to read the volumes from which those included here were chosen.

Midrash Rabbah, translated by H. Freedman (London: Soncino Press, 1939), is a ten-volume translation of midrashim on a variety of books of the Bible. There references here, which have been paraphrased and adapted, are to chapter and section. The third edition of this work was published in 1983.

Volume one in Louis Ginzberg's classic collection of stories related to biblical texts, *The Legends of the Jews,* translated by Henrietta Szold (Philadelphia: The Jewish Publication Society, 1909 and 1937), still in print, draws from a wide number of sources, including Christian and Islamic traditions. Here this work, again paraphrased and adapted, is listed as Ginzberg, followed by the volume and page number.

A wonderful addition to the library of persons interested in midrashim is

Rabbi William G. Braude's translation of Hayim Naham Bialik and Yehoshua Hana Ravnitzky's *The Book of Legends (Sefer Ha-Aggadah): Legends from the Talmud and Midrash*. References to this work are cited as *Sefer Ha-Aggadah*, followed by the page number and section number.

One more word on midrash: For any given passage of Scripture, several stories or interpretations of various rabbis are presented side by side in collections of midrashim. Those who collected these stories saw no reason to decide which was the one right interpretation. This is also true, we might mention, of those who assembled the canon of the New Testament, who saw no reason to choose among the four very different stories about Rabbi Jesus. The understanding behind these choices is that there need be no single correct interpretation. The Bible is viewed as being so inclusive that it could apply to a range of possible life situations. Therefore, we would expect a variety of interpretations to speak to a variety of life situations. Not only the Bible, but also all of its many possible interpretations, are encompassed by the expansive imagination of God. In fact, Solomon, the wisest of all humans, is reputed by the rabbis to have known three thousand stories for every verse of Scripture and one thousand and five interpretations for every story.

Learning to Tell Bible Stories

A Self-directed Workshop

1. Read the story aloud at least twice. You may choose to read the translation included here or the one you are accustomed to reading. I recommend that you examine at least two translations as you prepare, so you can hear the differences in the way they sound when read aloud.

Do read them *aloud*. Yes, if you are not by yourself, people may give you funny looks, but this really is important. Your ear will hear things about the passage that your eye will miss. Besides, you can't skim when you read aloud. You are forced to take your time, and you might notice aspects of the story that you never saw (or heard) before.

As you read, pay special attention to *where* the story takes place, *when* the story takes place, *who* the characters are, *what* objects are important to the story, and the general *order of events* in the story.

2. Now close your eyes and imagine the story taking place. This is your chance to become a playwright/director or screenwriter/filmmaker because you will experience the story on the stage or screen in your imagination. Enjoy this part of the process. It takes only a few minutes, and the budget is within everybody's reach.

3. Look back at the story briefly to make sure you haven't left out any important people, places, things, or events.

4. Try telling the story. This works better if you have someone to listen (even the family pet will do). You can try speaking aloud to yourself or to an imaginary listener. Afterward ask your listener or yourself what questions arise as a result of this telling. Is the information you need about the people, places, things, or language in the story? Is it appropriate to the age, experiences, and interests of those who will be hearing it? Does the story capture your imagination? One more thing: You don't have to be able to explain the meaning of a story to tell it. In fact, those of the most enduring interest have an element of mystery about them.

5. Read the "Comments on the Story" that Sharon Hels has provided for each passage. Are some of your questions answered there? You may wish also to look at a good Bible dictionary for place names, characters, professions, objects, or worlds that you need to learn more about. *The Interpreter's Dictionary of the Bible* (Nashville: Abingdon Press, 1962) is still the most complete source for storytellers.

21

6. Read the "Retelling the Story" section for the passage you are learning to tell. Does it give you any ideas about how you will tell the story? How would you tell it differently? Would you tell it from another character's point of view? How would that make it a different story? Would you transfer it to a modern setting? What places and characters will you choose to correspond to those in the biblical story? Remember, the retellings that are provided are not meant to be told exactly as they are written here. They are to serve as springboards for your imagination as you develop your telling.

7. Read the midrashim that accompany each retelling. Would you include any of these in your telling? You could introduce them by saying, "This is not in the original story, but the rabbis say. . . . " Do these midrashim respond to any of your questions or relate to any of your life situations or those of your listeners? If so, you might consider using them after the retelling to encourage persons to tell their own stories, which hearing the Bible story has brought to mind. You may even wish to begin creating some modern midrashim of your own or with your listeners.

8. Once you have gotten the elements of the story in mind and have chosen the approach you are going to take in retelling it, you need to practice, practice, practice. Tell the story aloud ten or twenty or fifty times over a period of several days or weeks. Listen as you tell your story. Revise your telling as you go along. Remember that you are not memorizing a text; you are preparing a living event. Each time you tell the story, it will be a little different, because you will be different (if for no other reason than that you have told the story before).

9. The "taste and see" that even the stories of God are good—not all sweet, but good and good for us and for those who hunger to hear.

I. Proverbs:

A Narrative Introduction

Introduction to the Book of Proverbs

The book of Proverbs is a literary monument to education in ancient Israel. This means education in the broadest sense: a fitting subtitle would be "The Book of Perpetual Teaching and Learning." As we read in Proverbs 1:45, the wisdom contained there will benefit both fools and wise, for everyone can increase in wisdom and understanding. Education as represented in Proverbs is not graded for difficulty or directed toward one group or another. Despite the fact that individual proverbs arose in different circumstances in Israelite culture, the sages ultimately made Israel's best insights available to one and all, making teachers and students of everyone.

Teachers and students appear in many guises. A mother and father, a queen, an Egyptian wise man—all these figures are various personae of the Israelite sage. The sages never signed their work or attempted to take credit for it individually. Yet over many centuries it is they who lovingly crafted, borrowed, and collected sayings and instructions for the benefit of their students—the ones they knew and those in later generations whom they would never know. Likewise, the unspecified student may be envisioned as a youth in an Israelite clan or someone far older, perhaps a thoughtful middle-aged man at the height of his abilities. She may have been the head of a large household or an old but vigorous woman. He may have acquired learning to represent his family at the court in Jerusalem or he may have been in training to become a scribe. All of these persons represent the Israelite (and later, Jewish) learner, who aspired to live with reverence toward God, decency toward others, and enlightened self-interest.

In addition to being directed toward everyone, wisdom addresses life as a whole. Again the introductory statement of the book indicates the compass of the subject matter of Proverbs: instruction, yes, but also the comprehension of wise words, a keen mind, righteousness, justice, and discernment. In short, to attain the final goal of education in Israel, one must become a person of integrity who takes the proper pathway in life, which is summarized by one essential statement: "The fear of the LORD is the beginning of wisdom." The Hebrew word for "beginning" can also mean "most important thing."

Proverbs is the proper starting point for examining the wisdom passages in the common lectionary because it is the heart of Israelite wisdom. Although the word *wisdom* occurs elsewhere in the Hebrew Bible, its meaning is not strictly identical to the basic educational stance to which we have referred. For instance, in the historical books, widom refers to the skill and artistry of the craftsman; in the prophetic books, the word *wisdom* may connote the specialized knowledge of foreign peoples. But if we are to understand wisdom as a phenomenon in ancient Israel, we must reckon first with the book of Proverbs, becoming familiar with its composition and asking questions as to how and under what conditions it arose as distinctive literature.

It may be helpful to begin with the smallest individual portion of wisdom literature before we look at the larger picture. At the molecular level, wisdom consists of two different forms that have recognizable subtypes. First is the *sentence,* constructed of two statements set parallel to each other. The sentence is often called a proverb. In the Hebrew text, each proverb looks like a single line of poetry with a clearly defined middle point. Like all Hebrew poetry, the relationship between the two halves is assessed in two ways, in terms of both meaning and word play (e.g., puns and repetition of sounds or rhythms in words). Subcategories of sentences include particular parallelism, the second half of the proverb reinforces the first. In antithetical parallelism, there is opposition between the two, so that the word *but* either appears or makes the best sense of what follows in the second half. There is a great store of antithetical proverbs in chapters 10–15. Two other forms are the comparison, usually called the "better" proverbs, and the unusual numerical proverbs, which use lists of things to draw comparisons (see Prov. 30:15-31). Numerical proverbs may be related to riddles (for a good example of a riddle, see Judges 14).

The other significant category of wisdom in Proverbs is the *instruction,* a designation that relates as much to its literary form as it does to its purpose, although the sentence also had a clear educational purpose. As opposed to the sentence, however, which is short and succinct, instructions are longer thematic poems with strong tones of admonition and warning. Scholars have pointed to the instructional material in Egyptian wisdom literature as a possible source for the Israelite variety of this form. Of the eight lections drawn from Proverbs that we will consider here, only 22:1-2, 8-9 and 25:6-7 are not instructions. The instructional material is probably not as well known as certain proverbs, so the selection in the Common Lectionary allows us to become familiar with some interesting new texts.

But the book of Proverbs is not just a selection of proverbs (and instructions, of course) from ancient Israel; rather, it is a library of proverb collections. Scholars disagree as to the exact number, but most cite four major collections, each beginning with its own heading: 1:1 (covering chaps. 1-9); 10:1 (covering chaps. 10–22:16); 22:17 (covering 22:17–24:34); and 25:1 (covering chaps.

25–29). There are also minor collections, including chapter 30 (the Sayings of Agur); 31:1-9 (the Sayings of Lemuel given to him by his mother); and finally the ode to the worthy woman in 31:10-30. The reader of Proverbs has several options for moving through the book. He or she can concentrate on one section, or can step back and look at the book as having been deliberately arranged in its final form. The collections can then be thought of as building blocks that create a greater structure of proverbial wisdom. For example, the ode to the good wife in 31:10-31 is usually considered a short hymn appended to the end of major collections. If we look at the structure of Proverbs as a whole, however, its position at the end of the book makes it the special conclusion of the entire book.

We have suggested that a series of anonymous sages wrote, collected, or borrowed the material in Proverbs over a long period of time. Authorship in the sense of the individual composition of original material that is the author's "intellectual property" does not really apply to the book of Proverbs. This includes authorship by Solomon, which most scholars reject. The Deuteronomic history records that Solomon was the sponsor of wisdom in Israel. This is still a useful tradition, even if the tradition of Solomonic authorship is not. Solomon was undoubtedly an intellectually gifted person whose acumen in statehood was renowned in his day throughout the ancient Near East. The stories of Solomon's inner piety (1 Kings 3:4-15), his discernment in judgment (1 Kings 3:16-28), and his leadership in wisdom among surrounding peoples (1 Kings 10:1-13) were preserved by the historians and make fascinating reading. The storyteller who wants to create an inviting biblical frame for his or her own wisdom stories may evoke the memory of Solomon by retelling these stories. In a sense, that is exactly what the Israelite sages did: In honor of Solomon's position as Israel's wisest king, the figure of Solomon turns up again and again in the wisdom literature.

Furthermore, the connection between the Israelite monarchy and the wisdom literature is vital. It is likely that at least some of the collections now included in the book of Proverbs have their origin during the time when Israel was organized as a state, whether a single unified state or two states (Judah and Israel), roughly from 1000–600 BCE. It was during that span of over four hundred years that the need for administrators and courtiers was great and the potential for contact with foreign sources of wisdom was high. The "men of Hezekiah" who copied out the proverbs found in chapters 25–29 may fall into this category. Sages may well have taken their place as advisers, secretaries, planners, and even historians and collectors of the old Israelite laws and stories. They would have given some thought to ideas that would reinforce the privileges and responsibilities of kingship and the state. The royal setting for wisdom will dictate a certain perspective on the wisdom literature. It may lead us to think of wisdom as an occupation of the cultural elite in Israel. In their hands, wisdom would have political overtones of the establishment rather than reform. For them, a sense of order and control was necessary for the smooth running of the affairs of state.

An alternative to the court setting of wisdom is the ancient clan structure of Israel. In time-honored tradition, generations were raised to maturity by the wisdom of the father, the absolute head of the household. Women had authority in the home over their young children, both male and female; a mother's word was considered authoritative. The additional role for male heads of households was a public one. The powerful heads of local clans, or "elders," took their places at the city gate to mediate disputes and render judgments for the common good. With an emphasis on the Israelite family, wisdom looks slightly different; it is geared toward the young person who has not yet taken up public responsibilities, and it may be more concerned with inner motivation to do good and protect the stability of the family rather than the strict regulation of manners.

There is one further option for the social setting of wisdom: the school. Although the Hebrew expression for a school, the *beit ha-midrash*, or house of study, is not mentioned in biblical literature, and indeed appears only in the book of Sirach (ca. 180 BCE), it is difficult to imagine any society maintaining its cultural continuity over the centuries as Israel did without educational institutions. Then as now, however, education could take place without the benefit of an actual school building. In ancient Israel, students may have been instructed in an informal public space, such as a quiet corner of the marketplace or a room at the Temple or at the home of a community leader. We, then, should imagine wisdom as being concerned with the development of skills and piety at all levels of intellectual development, including basic literacy, professional training, theological speculation, and the skillful composition of proverbs.

The truth is that all three of these settings probably contributed to the production of the book of Proverbs, for the sage belongs in all three camps. As anthropologists remind us, societies are complex, and isolating one aspect or another is likely to create an artificial picture of the whole. Rather than forcing ourselves to decide where a particular passage must have come from before we can work with it, we might instead see the confusion of social settings as evidence of the unity of Israelite society and how wisdom seemed to play an important part in all of Israelite life. And, too, it may be helpful for the storyteller to try to visualize one setting or another, or even experiment with different settings for the same text, to see which seems the most natural context for the material. Once this creative visualization takes place, storytellers may feel freer to provide their own narratives to coordinate with the texts—or to use the texts as launching pads for something completely new.

The religious orientation in the wisdom literature may seem remote or unusual to the reader at first, so a word about wisdom spirituality is called for. Because it was included with the religious literature of Israel, we should expect the wisdom literature to supplement, not contradict, the rest of the biblical canon. Indeed, since Proverbs orients us to the religious issues in Israelite wisdom literature as a whole, it gives us a more complete view of Israelite piety. Here we are in a somewhat different religious sphere than the one that is set forth in Genesis through Deuteronomy and the prophets. In fact, Proverbs contains no references to Israel's covenantal relationship with Yahweh. Instead it depends on two distinctive features: the counsel of the wise and an understanding of God as creator and sustainer of the universe.

The counsel of the wise (Hebrew, *etsah*) was not merely a suggestion or even a proposal to be debated. Instead, it was given and received with overwhelming seriousness, as a word of power. The counsel of the wise had the same authority as the word of the prophet or the Torah of the priest, as we see in Jeremiah 18:18. Of the royal counselor Ahithophel, 2 Samuel records that "in those days a man would seek counsel of Ahithophel as if he were making an enquiry of the word of God" (16:23). The counsel of the sage derived its authority from God's wisdom, which was supreme. For wisdom was a divine property, belonging to God's person and existing in itself God alone knows where (see Job 28). Wisdom does not belong to humankind as a possession, but human beings participate in wisdom to the extent that they bring themselves into conformity with its ways. The refrain in Proverbs 1-9, "The fear of the LORD is the beginning of wisdom," is a good summary of this piety, because in this phrase the sages expressed their belief that a proper awe and devotion toward God was both the beginning and the best part of wisdom.

Yahweh's wisdom manifests itself in the world fundamentally in terms of order—in nature and in the affairs of men and women. In nature, God is seen as the creator and maintainer of the entire cosmos, including the earth, sun and stars, the seasons, and plants and animals of all kinds, including human beings. Divine wisdom is structured into the cosmos, as Proverbs 3:19-20 and 8:22-31 show. These passages should be understood as creation stories to be compared with the better-known versions in Genesis 1–2. Human beings participate in that order and do their part to uphold it by living in a way that honors God as creator of all, rich and poor, and by organizing and framing their experiences in the form of proverbs and instruction that serve others. In this way the sages worshiped a God of love and compassion.

God's ordering of the cosmos has another side for human beings, and this is the system of reward and punishment called retribution. God the compassionate creator is also concerned with justice. God's wisdom is righteousness and justice, and those who ignore it follow the path of wickedness and folly. God established this arrangement and reinforces it with reward and punishment according to the choices human beings make in their lives:

By uprightness the blameless keep their course,
    but the wicked are brought down by their own wickedness. (11:5)

No mischief will befall the righteous
    but the wicked get their fill of adversity. (12:21)

While this "system" was susceptible to a rigid application in human events, so that person's misfortune was taken as evidence that he or she had sinned (as in the case of Job and his friends), the original intent of retribution as a concept was not that it would be used as an aid to human prejudice and small-mindedness. Retribution simply claims that God participates in the life choices human beings make, and that consistent good or evil will eventually see its just reward. For all the dangers here, there is something inherently satisfying and even comforting in such a world view, as fans of "Western" movies know.

Lady Wisdom Appears

Wisdom calls out a warning to all who will listen.

The Story

Wisdom cries aloud in the open air, and raises her voice in public places. She calls at the top of the bustling streets; at the approaches to the city gates she says: "How long will you simple fools be content with your simplicity? If only you would respond to my reproof, I would fill you with my spirit and make my precepts known to you. But because you refused to listen to my call, because no one heeded when I stretched out my hand, because you rejected all my advice and would have none of my reproof, I in turn shall laugh at your doom and deride you when terror comes, when terror comes like a hurricane and your doom approaches like a whirlwind, when anguish and distress come upon you. "The insolent delight in their insolence; the stupid hate knowledge. When they call to me, I shall not answer; when they seek, they will not find me. Because they detested knowledge and chose not to fear the LORD, because they did not accept my counsel and spurned all my reproof, now they will eat the fruits of their conduct and have a surfeit of their own devices; for simpletons who turn a deaf ear come to grief, and the stupid are ruined by their own complacency. But whoever listens to me will live without a care, undisturbed by fear of misfortune."

Comments on the Story

The Hebrew Bible uses the word *wisdom (hokmah)* in many ways, none of which provides an explicit definition of the term. This surely was no accident. The ancient Israelites seemed to understand that wisdom defied usual categories. Wisdom was not just a moral code or a set of principles. That would have limited its significance to human beings. Instead, claimed the sages, wisdom was present in all of creation, which was the work of God, whose power was without limit. The elusive quality of wisdom is grasped only by God, who alone knows its source, as the poet of Job declared (Job 28:23-28).

But the sages did not resort to abstractions when describing wisdom to their students. Instead, they chose among three options: First, they couched it in the form of astute observation of the social and natural order, embedding it in the form of the proverb. Another alternative was to use the voice of the parent exhorting his or her son; elders were seen as the ultimate source of wisdom in the ancient world. Their third option was the most radical: They personified wisdom so that it could speak for itself, and the persona they chose was female. This figure is the most striking aspect of the first collection of the book of Proverbs, chapters 1–9.

Lady Wisdom addresses men and women in the course of their daily trans-actions in the streets, public squares, markets, busy corners, and city gates. The sage, therefore, describes wisdom as both accessible as public address and as elusive as the opposite sex. Endowed with the ambiguity of full personhood, Lady Wisdom is found in the midst of everday life, where thoughts turn into moral—or immoral—actions, actions become habits, and habits produce char-acter. This, in the end, is how the presence of lack of wisdom determines the fate of an individual.

The passages containing Lady Wisdom (1:20-33; 8:1-4, 22-31; 8:1-8, 19-24; 9:1-6) envision her supervising proper conduct of life in the city, taking over the job when parents, who might be associated with the countryside, have been left behind. Surrounded by those less scrupulous than himself, the young city dweller may be tempted to minimize his ethical risk. Wisdom's address sug-gests that every task, however significant or trifling, is subject to the demands of wisdom. Wisdom's location in the city may suggest also that those who come there to make their fortune should seek more profound riches:

> "How long will you simple fools be
> content with your simplicity?
> If only you would respond to my reproof,
> I would fill you with my spirit
> and make my precepts known to you."

The figure of wisdom is often compared to a prophet. Wisdom then emulates persons who are familiar sights on the city streets, using some of their tactics to attract attention and win adherents to her message. Examples are the "pouring out of spirit" (v. 23), reminiscent of the post-exilic prophecy in Isaiah and Joel, and the threat in verses 24-27, analogous to the promise of judgment by God for ignoring the demands of the covenant between God and Israel (Exodus 19–21). The passage ends with a promise of deliverance from misfortune to all who heed wisdom's advice (v. 33). Like the word of the Lord (Isa. 55:6-11), the word of wisdom has a purpose to fulfill. Human beings ignore it at their own peril.

But there are some important difficulties with the prophetic model. One, wisdom announces her own word, not the word of the Lord—and it is a word to the simple, to fools *(petayim),* not to Israel, its leaders, or the surrounding nations. While Yahweh may have initiated the mechanistic system of reward and punishment (retribution) that is common in wisdom literature, this point is not made directly. Wisdom merely offers to preserve the fool from fear and misfortune, but will laugh if her advice is ignored and trouble strikes. The prophet had no such option, but was answerable for the repentance of his people (see Ezekiel 3).

Behind this powerfully evocative figure of Lady Wisdom stands not the prophet, therefore, but the wisdom teacher. This teacher could have been based at the royal court in Jerusalem or at a separate school for the training of scribes. The court would have needed educated diplomats capable of negotiations on behalf of the state in its interests outside the country. Scribes, on the other hand, were needed for administrative tasks of all kinds, and would have required skills in drafting documents of all kinds, recording financial transactions, and the like.

Both court and scribal schools require a foundation in good character and behavior from students, which the instructions of Lady Wisdom seem meant to reinforce.

Wisdom's persona as a worthy woman has a great deal to do with the audience of her message. The main targets of her appeal are young, inexperienced males who are tasting their first responsibility in public life. (Fools, scoffers, simpletons, etc., may include young women, but these were the exceptions rather than the rule.) Like Abigail, whose brave actions and skillful words protected David from carrying out a foolish oath (1 Sam. 25:2-42), Lady Wisdom encounters young men on the street and tries to direct their energy to a positive purpose.

The personification of wisdom is powerful poetic stratagem for the sage. It allows the teacher to show the student that wisdom is encountered in relationship with one unlike oneself, through whom the most profound secrets of life can be mediated. These are the secret sources of success, and they are found when one has an attitude of openness and receptivity that allows learning and growth in character to take place. After hearing the call of the Lady, the student will pursue true wisdom and will never again confuse instruction with an indoctrination into dull conformity.

Retelling the Story

"Wisdom cries aloud in the open air, and raises her voice in public places." (Prov. 1:20)

My mother, who was the quintessential wise woman, often spoke in a loud voice to me, but only in our home, never in public places. She often spoke with proverbs, her gained folk wisdom, such as: "Don't spit in the river, there may come a time to drink"; "A mountain and a mountain cannot come together, but a person and a person can." And what she said, always in Yiddish, while offering me her wisdom and experience, was: "Foolish girl, be smart! Where is your common sense? Have sense!" And often she would follow these admonitions with a teaching tale. When I lost my temper, which was quite often apparently because I heard this story hundreds of times, she would tell me the following story, to teach me to restrain my anger:

> Rabbi Judah, the Patriarch, forbade his students to teach Torah in the hustle and bustle of the marketplace. When one of his disciples, Rabbi Hiyya, taught his nephews outside, his teacher was upset. When the student came to his rabbi, Judah told him that someone was calling him outside. At these words the student knew that his teacher had taken his infraction seriously. He stayed away for thirty days before he returned. When he came again to see his teacher, the elder rabbi asked why his student had ignored his prohibition to teach Torah outside. Hiyya answered that Proverbs says that wisdom cries aloud in the streets. His teacher retorted, "You have read the passage once but not twice. Or perhaps you have read it twice but not three times. Or, if you have read it three times, then you have not understood it properly. When Proverbs says that, it means that wisdom will proclaim the good deeds in the street of the one who studies Torah inside." (Sefer Ha-Aggadah, 264.298)

Once there was a couple who had a baby son. Soon after the birth of the child, the husband was forced to leave his home to fight in the Russian Army, and he was away for many many years.

One night, he returned home. Just as he was about to knock on the door, he heard voices in the house: first a man's deep voice and then his wife's voice answering. He could not hear their words, only their voices.

> The idea that we humans reject God's counsel means that we often stand in the way of the good things God has planned for us. When God wishes to bless we are not ready to receive a blessing. This leaves God to mourn for us in our lack of wisdom. (Numbers Rabbah 16.24 and Song of Songs Rabbah 8.5 [1])

The soldier-husband was infuriated at the thought that his wife was unfaithful and had taken a lover during his absence. In his rage, he drew his revolver and prepared to rush in and kill the man in his house. As he forced the door open, he suddenly heard the word "Mama" and he realized that the man was his son, now grown up. Fortunately, he had stopped himself in time.

The husband fell to his knees and begged his wife and son for forgiveness, shuddering over what he might have done.

The images from this story have stayed with me over the years. Only recently have I discovered that my grandmother told a similar story to a cousin when he was a child in order to teach him patience. All this time I had thought it a story my mother had heard somewhere, or a tale based on something that had actually happened in Russia. "How wonderful," I mused, "that this is a story my mother probably heard from her mother." What excitement I felt, then, when I discovered that a variant of this story is to be found in a thirteenth-century collection of ethical precepts and folktales called *Sefer Hasidim (Book of the Pious)*, assembled by Reb Yehuda Hahasid.

The wisdom of "restraint of anger" and other wisdoms for sale can be found in folktales. And if the seller is not King Solomon, it is Elijah, or else a wise old woman, a Lady Wisdom. (*Peninnah Schram*)*

*Originally published as "How to Restrain Your Anger," in *Jewish Stories One Generation Tells Another*, by Peninnah Schram.

PROVERBS 8:1-4, 22-31

Lady Wisdom's Noble Birth

Wisdom is the first of all that God created—but now she's for sale.

The Story

Hear how wisdom calls and understanding lifts her voice. She takes her stand at the crossroads, by the wayside, at the top of the hill; beside the gate, at the entrance to the city, at the approach by the portals she cries aloud: "It is to you I call, to all mankind I appeal:

· ·

"The LORD created me the first of his works long ago, before all else that he made. I was formed in earliest times, at the beginning, before earth itself. I was born when there was yet no ocean, when there were no prings brimming with water. Before the mountains were settled in their place, before the hills I was born, when as yet he had made neither land nor streams nor the mass of the earth's soil. When he set the heavens in place I was there, when he girdled the ocean with the horizon, when he fixed the canopy of clouds overhead and confined the springs of the deep, when he prescribed limits for the sea so that the waters do not transgress his command, when he made earth's foundations firm. Then I was at his side each day, his darling and delight, playing in his presence continually, playing over his whole world, while my delight was in mankind."

Comments on the Story

As the sages of Israel probed the depths of life they allowed their metaphorical creation, Lady Wisdom, to express their most mystical insights. Once again, Lady Wisdom asks for an audience at the portals of the city, but now her message is a universal one. The student may now be a middle-aged man at the height of his powers, who sees the prizes of power and wealth that his ambition teaches him to crave. Lady Wisdom does not disparage these prizes. Instead, she claims that her benefits outweigh these things, and that in fact they are gifts for her to bestow at her own pleasure. Are we to believe that a woman who stands and calls to passers-by on the street exercises control over the destinies of all humankind, even the richest and most powerful? To convey her majesty, the sages have composed a poem about wisdom and her role in creation (vv. 22-31). Proverbs 8:22-31 is one of the few truly mystical passages in the Hebrew Bible, rivaling the dual creation stories in Genesis 1–2. Wisdom describes the

34

universe into which she came forth (if not the actual circumstances of her birth) in verses 22-26. We can only infer that this is the site of creation at the point when "the spirit of God [was] moving across the face of the deep" (Gen. 1:2); something more than chaos but less than fully configured nature, before the grossest elements of the natural world were put into their permanent positions. Then wisdom was "born"—a being with a female presence coming somehow from Yahweh, a being with a predominantly male presence. One thinks of the ancient Greek deity Athena (Roman, Minerva), the warrior goddess associated with wisdom, springing full-grown from the forehead of her father, Zeus, or Adam "giving birth" to Eve. The remainder of the poem describes her relationship to the deity as the world was being made. Since the relationship centers on Wisdom's witness of creation as it happened, it can be considered an additional creation story. First God fixed the boundaries between sky and water, and then made the earth a solid platform. These are the building blocks that God created, according to the priestly writer, on the first three days (minus the earth's vegetation). Wisdom is not a female creator, but her privileged position (as royal princess, one of several possible meanings for the word *amon* in v. 30, where the REB translates "darling") gives her privileged understanding; what she saw was instantly incorporated into joyful awareness.

In offering the pedigree of wisdom and its foundation in the creation of the world, the sages have something important to convey to their student.

Some interpreters have seen evidence in this passage of an Israelite goddess of wisdom. This suggestion cannot be dismissed; other ancient Near Eastern religions contain references to wisdom as one of the deities (Egypt, Ma'at; Babylon, Ishtar or Siduri Sabitu; Canaan, El). But the comparison alone is not sufficient to establish Lady Wisdom as a goddess. Further questions remain: Was Hebrew religion monotheistic, early enough in its history, to make Wisdom simply an attribute of God? Was there enough latitude in Israelite religion to tolerate sub-deities who might also be worshiped? No one knows for sure— although there are some tantalizing clues, including in the post-exilic era a goddess-worshiping Jewish community outside Palestine in the Egyptian settlement of Elephantine.

The mythic background of Lady Wisdom and her relationship to Yahweh finds an interesting analogy in modern Christianity. Like Judaism, Christianity formally rejects polytheism. Despite the strictly delimited trinitarian concepts expressed in the creeds, however, theologians (lay and ordained, academic and intuitive) have throughout the history of the church used nontraditional images to express their new ideas, images, and understandings of God's nature, which, after all, may not be limited by human categories. The storyteller might grant that these ideas have not been given their own personality, nor do they claim the authority of Scripture. But originally, neither did the sage who composed these lovely poems.

The creation of Lady Wisdom is best understood as a metaphor that conveys theological truth to Israel using image, intrigue, and the power of the imagination at the service of God. Metaphor is not just flowery or elevated speech. Instead, it is the mating of two distinct elements, each with its own associations in human experience, to form a lively new entity. Lady Wisdom is such a being. A solitary, mysterious, and yet beneficent figure, she calls her hearers to make use of their imaginations to apprehend her truth. This truth is expressed both in her being and in her message: the independent yet attainable quality of wisdom, one of God's noblest blessings on humankind. Lady Wisdom, therefore, partakes of a reality no less potent in the Israelite mind than that of God's relationship with Israel in history.

Retelling the Story

"She takes her stand at the crossroads, by the wayside, at the top of the hill; beside the gate, at the entrance to the city." (Prov. 8:2-3)

In a small village, in a certain country, there once lived a husband and wife. Although they worked very hard, there was never enough food, never enough money for clothes, and certainly never enough for *tzedaka* (charity); there were so many charity funds in the village—for the poor, for penniless brides, for the old, for the synagogue.

Some rabbis say that the Hebrew word describing a playing child present at the creation with God could also be the word for an architect's drawings. They say that wisdom was the design for the universe that existed in God's imagination before anything was created. Just as someone building a house doesn't build it room by room without a plan, so also an architect does not work without a design in mind; just so God had wisdom (or the Torah) as the ideal design for the universe and all that is in it. *(Genesis Rabbah, 1.1)*

Early one morning, the husband decided to journey far away from home and try to earn enough money so that when he returned in a year or two, they would have a more comfortable life and perhaps even have enough for *tzedaka*.

And so he traveled and worked, worked and traveled farther and farther from home. Finally, after eighteen years of hard work, he had saved three bags full of money—one filled with gold coins, one with silver coins, and one with copper coins—and he started on his return home.

On the way, he came to a town where a fair was underway. "Perhaps I will be able to buy something for my wife," he thought. So he began to walk through the fair in search of an unusual gift. He examined all kinds of objects and listened to the various merchants sing the praises of their wares, but he found nothing that pleased him.

As he was about to leave the fair grounds, the man noticed an old woman sitting quietly, with a large beautifully woven shawl on her lap.

"That shawl pleases me," said the man. "How much does it cost?"

"No, no, this shawl is not for sale," answered the woman. "What, then, do you sell? Are you not a merchant too?" asked the man.

"I am a merchant, but I sell something unusual—not the customary fare, for not everyone wants to buy what I see," replied the old woman, smiling.

"You speak in riddles, good woman," said the man. "But I am looking for the unusual to bring as a gift to my wife. So perhaps I will be the right customer for you."

"In that case, I will tell you. I sell wise sayings," the old woman said.

"Wise sayings?" asked the man in surprise. "And how much do you charge for this wisdom?"

"A bag of copper coins," answered the old woman.

Fascinated by what he had heard, the man handed the bag of copper coins to the old woman and said, "Tell me what wise sayings this bag of coins buys."

The old woman put the bag of coins in her shawl and told the man, "Always follow the main road, though it take longer."

The man waited for the important piece of wisdom. When he realized that the saying was all there was, he turned to the old woman and said, "But where is the wisdom?"

"You will see," answered the old woman. "This advice will be useful someday."

The man now became even more curious and said, "Here is a bag of silver coins. Sell me more wisdom."

"Very well," answered the old woman. Taking the bag of silver coins and carefully placing it in her shawl, she said, "What is called ugly is also beautiful."

Now the man was even more confused. "You speak in riddles but I am not Solomon," cried the man. "My two bags of coins, which took me so many years to earn, have been given up for two useless riddles."

Even though he wanted to leave, to run away from this place, the man was more than ever intrigued by the old woman, and he thought, "Maybe, just maybe, I can get some wisdom from her that will really help me."

And so, the man told the old woman that he had one more bag, a bag filled with gold coins. "Sell me something worthy of this gold," he pleaded.

And the old woman took the bag of gold and replied: "Beware of anger in the evening—but rather wait until morning."

The man turned away, not knowing whether to be angry or sad—and when he turned back to where the old woman had been, there was only a basket with a loaf of bread and the beautiful shawl. The man began to cry, "What have I done? I've given away my hard-earned fortune for three sayings. What shall I do now?" Mumbling miserably to himself, he decided to take the shawl he had admired so much and the bread.

As he gathered up the shawl, he noticed it was heavy, heavier than such a shawl normally is. To his surprise, he found the three bags of coins wrapped up in the shawl. He looked around for the old woman, but she was nowhere to be found. When he inquired about the old woman, the other merchants laughed at him, "What old woman? You must be crazy."

Puzzled by the disappearance of the intriguing old woman but joyful about his restored earnings, the man continued on his way home.

He walked a long way, and when he had grown tired and hungry he stopped on the side of the road to eat. As he was eating a piece of the old woman's bread, two carriages carrying merchants came down the road. Seeing this lone traveler, the merchants stopped and invited him to ride with them to the next town. The man accepted the offer gladly.

As they were driving along, they came to a divided path. Both roads led to the same town, but the path on the left was shorter. As the merchants were about to go to the left, the man riding in the carriage suddenly noticed the shawl in his pack, and he recalled the first piece of advice the old woman had sold him, "Always follow the main road though it may take longer."

The man stood up and shouted for the drivers to stop. When he directed them to stay on the main highway, the merchants began to argue with him. Only when he was about to step down from the carriage did the merchants in his carriage agree. The merchants in the other carriage, however, refused to travel the longer distance. They were anxious to get to the next town and sell their goods.

When the man and his fellow passengers reached the town, they discovered that the other carriage had not yet arrived. "Perhaps they had a broken wheel or, even worse, were held up by robbers," the merchants said.

"We must go help them," insisted the man. So they got back into the carriage and returned along the shorter path. As they entered a wooded area, they saw that robbers had indeed stopped the second carriage. When the robbers saw the first carriage approaching, they fled into the woods. The merchants were so grateful to the traveler that they gave him a bag of gold coins and wished him godspeed on his way home.

A few weeks later, the man was about to enter a big city. Wherever he walked, he heard people laughing at their once powerful and beloved King.

Wherever he looked, he saw people looting and robbing, since they no longer held any regard for the King's laws.

When he entered the courtyard of the King's palace, he saw all the servants and guards pushing and poking at a shriveled-up man who looked more like a wild animal than a human being. He had an oversized head and bumps and scales growing everywhere on his body. His hands and feet were twisted, and his voice was no longer a human-sounding voice but sounded more like the cry of a wounded animal. Everyone was shouting, "Get away, you ugly beast! Of course you are a King—the King of ugliness!" They kept taunting and chiding this creature.

When the traveler came closer for a good look at the tortured man, he remembered the advice of the old woman: "What is called ugly is beautiful."

"Yes," he shouted, "You are beautiful, for everything that God has created is beautiful."

When these words were spoken, the shriveled-up man was suddenly transformed, and he became the handsome, tall King he had once been. With tears of gratitude, he thanked the traveler and told him how a demon had put a curse on him. Only when someone would call him beautiful could the curse be lifted. And because the traveler had saved the kingdom, the King gave him many bags of gold and jewels and the clothes of a nobleman.

When the man finally arrived in his own village, night had fallen and he did not want to frighten his wife at such a late hour. Instead, he went to an inn nearby. As he was led to his room, he noticed that the servant was his own wife. But she did not seem to recognize him. She looked at him but without a smile of recognition.

The husband's joy turned instantly to disappointment. "Could it be because of my rich clothes? Have I changed so much?" He sat in the room, becoming more and more upset and angry.

"What! I traveled and worked thinking only of returning to my wife and my home—and now here I am and my own wife has forgotten me!"

The anger struck at him in torrents and he hastily picked up his bags, determined to leave town and never to return. As he did so, the shawl dropped out, and the man remembered the third bit of wisdom he had bought: "Beware of anger in the evening—but rather wait until morning."

And so the man restrained his anger and waited impatiently—but he waited until it was light.

In the morning, as he was about to leave, the servant, his wife, met him at the door and she exclaimed, "Excuse me, sir, if I stared at you last evening, for you reminded me of someone I once knew."

"And who is that?" asked the man.

"It was my husband, who left here eighteen years ago," she replied softly. "I fear he must be dead, for I have received no news of him for many years, but it is hard to forget someone you love."

"My dear wife," said the man, "forgive me for not telling you who I was last night. I thought you had forgotten me. I have returned to you, and with good fortune besides."

And so the husband and wife were reunited, and they lived in happiness,

The rabbis say that God has taste and even food as a part of the divine being. In the Psalms it is written, "Taste and see that the Lord is good." In this passage in Proverbs God speaks of having fruit, this divine delicacy being the fruit of wisdom. *(Exodus Rabbah* 17.2)

with wisdom and wealth for the rest of their lives. *(Peninnah Schram)**

*Originally published as "Wisdom for Sale," in *Jewish Stories One Generation Tells Another*, by Peninnah Schram.

Fools and Truth; Wisdom and Wealth

Wisdom is better than great riches, and all who are simple can learn from her.

The Story

Hear how wisdom calls and understanding lifts her voice. She takes her stand at the crossroads, by the wayside, at the top of the hill; beside the gate, at the entrance to the city, at the approach by the portals she cries aloud: "It is to you I call, to all mankind I appeal: understand, you simpletons, what it is to be shrewd; you stupid people, understand what it is to have sense. Listen! For I shall speak clearly, you will have plain speech from me; for I speak nothing but truth, and my lips detest wicked talk. All that I say is right, not a word is twisted or crooked.

. . . .
My harvest is better even than fine gold, and my revenue better than choice silver. I follow the course of justice and keep to the path of equity. I endow with riches those who love me; I shall fill their treasuries."

. . . .
She says to him who lacks sense, "Come, eat the food I have prepared and taste the wine that I have spiced. Abandon the company of simpletons and you will live, you will advance in understanding."

Comments on the Story

This poem, a composite of various segments of chapters 8 and 9, allows us to concentrate on other aspects of Lady Wisdom's addressees and, indeed, her rival.

In this passage, Wisdom seeks to match her gifts with the appropriate persons. The Hebrew terms for simpletons *(p'tayim)* and stupid people *(k'silim)* are significant here. The label does not apply to those who are lacking in intelligence but to those who are callously indifferent to the needs of others, whose speech and behavior serves only their own narrowly defined interests. They may affect sophistication and *savoir faire*, but they are morally dead. Naturally, they will not seek out Lady Wisdom themselves. So Lady Wisdom calls to them, offering "shrewdness and sense"—a very telling combination of traits. The word translated "shrewd" is *'ormah*. This is "cleverness," or even "cun-

41

ning," words that carried the same moral ambiguity then as they do now. The serpent in the Garden of Eden, for example, was "the most cunning of all the creatures" (Gen. 3:1). The quality of shrewdness might just appeal to the *p'tayim* and *k'silim,* who would want to maintain the appearance of control. But Lady Wisdom then qualifies its meaning with another term: *sense,* which is literally "an understanding heart" *(habinu leb).* The heart was the organ of reason in ancient Israel, which associated parts of the body with aspects of consciousness. Wisdom is specifically dissociated from "wicked talk." In verse 12 (not part of our reading) wicked talk appears with arrogance, pride, and evil ways.

The morally indifferent, or foolish/stupid ones, therefore, are to learn from Lady Wisdom that truthfulness is the essential currency of human relationships. They are to emulate her disciplined speech, which is one component of the disciplined life she advocates. Speech carries profound significance in the Israelite wisdom tradition, as it does in prophecy and worship. The two extremes of human speech, its suppression in silence and its flowering in poetry, are both present in this literature. In between lies the golden mean of the honest word spoken at the right time. Honesty and straightforwardness are the foundations of justice, which is Wisdom's "harvest." The agricultural reference harkens back to the teaching on retribution: You will reap exactly what you sow. This metaphor for actions and their consequences runs through both the Hebrew Bible and the New Testament.

The next segment of this passage permits us to consider the question of the relationship between prudent behavior and success. Can the wise expect to become rich as a result of their prudence? Is a prosperous life a sufficient sign of the possession of wisdom? These verses suggest it; wisdom literature in general gives a great deal of attention to the relation between prosperity and piety but does not give a unequivocal answer. The extremes include on the one hand Job, with his wealth and piety, who is considered the supreme innocent sufferer in the Hebrew Bible, and on the other hand, in the New Testament, the special condemnation of the rich in the book of James. The wisdom perspective on wealth is controlled by the observation of what it can do to human character. In the case of one already dedicated to wisdom, its influence is minimal; the social standing that often accompanies it implies certain responsibilities. But to one who has not dedicated oneself to the art of living wisely, wealth brings nothing but disaster; families are torn apart, social mores flaunted, and the heart harbors only despair.

The poet will not engage in such literal thinking here. In this passage, wisdom's riches are not silver or gold but justice and equity (lit., righteousness and justice). Wisdom endows her students with these advantages, not cold cash or securities. A truly wise individual will value justice and equity far more than personal wealth—for a society without justice is fundamentally disordered. And in that case no fortune is secure.

The final section of this reading echoes the language of Lady Wisdom's rival and competitor for the interest of the student, the so-called "strange woman" *(ishah zara/nokriyah).*

The strange woman is not a prostitute but an unfaithful wife who lures the foolish man into her house for illicit sexual relations (2:16-19; 5:3-14; 6:24-35; 7:6-27; 9:13-18). While the persuasiveness of the unfaithful wife is not excused—especially when she argues that punishment does not follow crime—the accent in these passages falls on the man's responsibility to avoid her house. For him, it is a clear-cut case of self-enhancement or self-destruction. In Israel, prostitutes were harshly censured, but men were not held accountable for consorting with them. The adulterous couple, however, threatened the family structure to its core; adultery, therefore, is the ultimate social chaos and can stand in for anarchy in general.

The strange woman in Proverbs, the negative foil for Lady Wisdom, can be compared to the prophets' use of negative female images to illustrate the broken nature of Yahweh's relationship with Israel: Hosea's marriage to Gomer, Ezekiel's poetic description of Jerusalem (chap. 16) and Oholah and Oholibah (chap. 23). In post-exilic Israel, the family and its stability became the focus of community solidarity (Mal. 2:13-16), to the extent that women represented the spiritual purity of Israel as a whole, and it was necessary to divorce foreign wives and disinherit "their" children to preserve the community (Ezra 10). In Proverbs, however, the foreign woman/adulteress is still a symbol of a man's opportunity to derail his life definitively. Heading in the opposite direction, to Lady Wisdom, promises life, security, prosperity—together with the joyful companionship of one's own spouse, who, as we shall see, is on the same journey herself (Proverbs 31).

Retelling the Story

"Listen! For I shall speak clearly, you will have plain speech from me; for I speak nothing but truth, and my lips detest wicked talk." (Prov. 8:6-7)

The questions of truth, and whose truth, and which roads leads to truth have been argued for centuries. Also the question of stories as truth or as distortion of truth (or even as lies) has also been an open discussion for generations. How do we best hear and understand truth? Perhaps through a story, after all, through the use of imagination. In other words, by concealing the truth with a "lie," we can best uncover truth. The story serves as the coating on the "philosophic pill." One who had such an approach was Rabbi Jacob Kranz, (1741–1804), the Maggid of Dubno. A maggid is an itinerant preacher/rabbi who taught Judaism through the use of parables. Let me tell you one of the Dubno Maggid's tales on the subject of Truth and Parable.

One day in a small town some of the members of the community approached the Maggid of Dubno and said:

"You are a great scholar and speaker. Your parables are also excellent. But, tell us, are they really necessary? We all know that Judaism is based on plain truth, so why obscure the actual facts with parables, beautiful as they are?"

> The rabbis relate the fruit of wisdom to the festivals that were observed at God's command. It was on the feast of the harvest that the Torah was given and thus its wisdom is fruit to nourish the faithful, just as the harvest brings in fruit to strengthen their bodies. Also at the feast of ingathering, the blessings of God are the fruit that is gathered into the homes of the faithful. *(Exodus Rabbah* 31.16)

The Maggid of Dubno replied, "Well, since we are talking about parables, let me answer your questions with a parable:

When people saw how Naked Truth used to walk about bare and unadorned in the town, they turned away in disgust and refused even to look at him. Wherever Truth went, he was rebuffed or, at best, ignored. One day, as Truth walked down a side street, he met a friend dressed in beautiful garments. It was none other than Parable. Now Truth poured out his bitter heart to Parable, and said: "Oh Parable, tell me why is it that you should receive so much attention, while I, the actual Truth, get none whatever?

Replied Parable: "The trouble, my friend, lies in the fact that you walk about plain and unadorned. No one likes to meet the naked Truth face to face. Let me help you and you will see a change for the better in your life." And, without waiting for an answer, Parable clothed him in some of her own garments, and behold, Truth looked most elegant and attractive.

> When the Bible speaks of walking in the way or path of righteousness, the rabbis say that one reference is to the Ten Commandments, which walks in the midst of the Torah like a fine and distinguished lady walks surrounded by those who look after her safety. *(Exodus Rabbah* 30.3)

From then on, wherever Truth appeared in his exquisite new apparel, he was greeted and welcomed most cordially, and he prospered in all his endeavors.

"This," concluded the Maggid of Dubno, "is what I try to do for truth through the parables. Truth will remain the same unalterable, with or without my parables. But most people cannot bear to come face-to-face with naked Truth. Therefore truth can often find its way into their hearts only when it is clothed in a parable. While the parable does nothing to change the truth, it makes it beautiful and appealing to those who would otherwise ignore it." (*Peninnah Schram*)

PROVERBS 9:1-6

The Hospitality of Lady Wisdom

Wisdom completes her house and declares a feast.

The Story

Wisdom has built her house; she has hewn her seven pillars. Now, having slaughtered a beast, spiced her wine, and spread her table, she has sent her maidens to proclaim from the highest point of the town: "Let the simple turn in here." She says to him who lacks sense, "Come, eat the food I have prepared and taste the wine that I have spiced. Abandon the company of simpletons and you will live, you will advance in understanding."

Comments on the Story

In this reading, Lady Wisdom appears in her full aristocratic glory. Instead of standing and calling in the street, she is now mistress of the palatial house she has built. Her servants will call guests to a sumptuous banquet she has prepared. Her hospitality enables young men to become wise and therefore to live a full, complete life. At the same time, however, her rival Lady Stupidity makes her pitch to young, inexperienced men. She sits at the door of her house and tells them about her food, which, although plain fare, is enhanced by secrecy and danger. In between these two major segments of the chapter lie several verses that intend to hold up a mirror to the young man so that he can recognize himself as either insolent, wise, arrogant, or righteous.

This passage, like previous passages concerning Lady Wisdom, shows how intertwined the various female roles in Proverbs 1–9 can be. Some scholars have argued that the new setting of Lady Wisdom at her house relies on the image of the strange woman, who does not stand on the street like Lady Wisdom but beckons young men into her home. Yet the building of a house, like the creation of the world, is something in which wisdom can claim original participation; the strange woman has no part in the story of origins, not even to symbolize the presence of original sin. The house is a microcosm for the universe, as the reference to seven pillars shows. The exact number of pillars is inconsequential, but the correspondence among universe/temple/house is useful for dramatizing the contrast between one home and another.

It is worth pointing out that the passage has overtones of foreign fertility practices, in which the devotees of the Goddess secure young men to carry out fertility rituals (i.e., sexual intercourse). But even this is no more than the scent of intrigue compared to the full-scale conspiracy of Lady Stupidity. Wisdom's banquet can also be compared to priestly sacrifice, where God's blessing is imparted to those who join in the sacred meal. But the sacramental aspect of this meal is symbolic. Sitting and eating a meal with Lady Wisdom is akin to the process of receiving instruction, which is like intellectual and moral nourishment. This is what gives the blessing of life, rather than spending time with dissolute companions, which holds no hope for positive change.

The real analog to Lady Wisdom and her house is the Worthy Woman in Proverbs 31. Lady Wisdom's house is a mythical dwelling, and the Worthy Woman's house is an idealized dwelling; but in an important sense, the Worthy Woman's house completes the metaphor because it becomes the symbol of social order as a whole. Lady Wisdom's house is only briefly sketched, but it is the model of stability and blessing that is used as a pattern for the blessing of the well-founded human household, which both creates and nourishes life. Both of these, in the poet's mind, are presided over by wise women. As Lady Wisdom engages in the activities of a homemaker, the Worthy Woman in her seemingly endless and detail-oriented daily activities is now endowed with the authority of Lady Wisdom. The two feminine figures bless each other with vitality.

Lady Stupidity's house, on the other hand, intensifies the portrait of the Strange Woman, who is alone in the house of her husband. The adulteress sets a trap for the young man with flattery and promises of great pleasure without negative consequences. She has abandoned her covenant with her husband and her God, and she is not at all concerned for the fate of her new partner. She is flighty and restless until she has found a victim to seduce. The poet promises that God will watch his ways and will repay him for the evil he has committed by deserting his own wife to embrace this beautiful, amoral woman. Lady Stupidity is all the things the adulteress in previous chapters is, but her speech is now not merely seductive but focused and proverbial as well. Her target is precisely the simple man, the one lacking in judgment *(hasar leb)* that Lady Wisdom calls. The image of eating is, of course, a sexual one, but her words incorporate the actions of wicked men as well—those who relish committing crimes, and who are restless unless they are plotting to murder and steal. Lady Stupidity evokes their presence with her words: "Stolen water is sweet, and bread eaten in secret tastes good." The fool thinks he is unique, but once in her house he finds himself among all those who have been duped by her appeal. He is in the house of the dead.

In the text, between the houses of Lady Wisdom and Lady Stupidity, stands the young man with an important decision to make. Gaining wisdom means enduring reproof, which is unpleasant but worthwhile in the long run. An insolent person cannot tolerate such treatment for any reason. Scholars have seen

46

verses 7-9 as an addition to this chapter, but they have their place as a comment on the first section. Do not mistake the imagery, this section seems to say; gaining wisdom is not as easy as sitting down to a sumptuous banquet. There is no such thing as a free lunch! Wisdom's meat and drink, although attractive enough, entail correction, lectures, and teaching. Verses 10-12, which have been understood by some as the actual conversation at Lady Wisdom's table (to extend the metaphor), are a reminder of what Lady Wisdom promises: long life and a perpetual gain in wisdom. It is possible that these verses were originally connected to Proverbs 9:1-6. The net effect of their current placement, however, is to let the poet reinforce his closing message that the reader faces an existential dilemma about the nature of his life. The house he enters will determine whether he lives a complete life and can die at peace or his life is cut short by alienation from his community and certain death. A man's home, therefore, is not just his castle—it is his destiny.

Retelling the Story

Wisdom has built her house. . . . "Abandon the company of simpletons and you will live, you will advance in understanding." (Prov. 9:1, 6)

In this wisdom story from the Middle East, one of the ten sons inherits something better than money, a legacy that reinforces the values our sages taught: "Acquire yourself a companion" (Ávot 1:6); and, as Ben Sirach advised: "There will be many who ask after your well-being, but reveal your secret only to one in a thousand."

Who could be happier than a man who has true wealth: children, friends, many good deeds to his credit, and, in addition, a treasure of many gold pieces? There once was such a man. He had acquired his gold through hard work and performing good deeds, and he was proud of all that he had accomplished.

One day, he called his ten sons close to him and told them, "My children, I will one day soon distribute my wealth among you while I still live. You will each receive 100 gold pieces. You should not have to wait for my death in order to benefit from this money. Even though I remain alive, you will have full control of the money and can use it in any way you please."

Time passed. But the wheel of fortune turned, and soon the man found himself with only 950 gold pieces left to him. He again called his ten sons to him and said, "My children, a great portion of my fortune has been lost, but I want to keep the promise that I made to you some time ago. I promised to give each of you 100 gold pieces and I can still do that, but for only nine of you. From the 50 remaining gold pieces I must keep 30 for myself and my burial expenses, and that leaves only 20 gold pieces for one of you.

"I am, as you know, blessed with ten good friends, companions of my youth,

> The rabbis contrast Wisdom's table to the table of those who lead others into foolishness. Those who would lead us astray also set a luscious banquet before the simple, giving many fine gifts to those who would follow them. But as soon as one joins with the foolish each one takes back whatever he or she had contributed to get the new convert. On the other hand, the gifts of Wisdom are lasting. *(Sefer Ha-Aggadah, 517.110)*

and they will be friends to the son who chooses to inherit the remaining 20 gold pieces. Since it is difficult for a parent to choose, I will ask you: Which one of you will volunteer to become the possessor of the 20 coins?"

The father looked at his sons, one by one. Each son in turn lowered his eyes and shook his head, indicating that he was not willing to accept the smaller inheritance. Finally, the father turned to his youngest son, and the one he loved the most, the child of his old age.

"Yes, Father, I will be content with the 20 gold pieces and I happily accept your offer," replied the youngest son as he lovingly embraced his father.

"Good," answered the father. "But know that my friends will be your companions, and they are worth more than gold and silver."

Within a short time after that, the father died. The sons observed the required seven days of mourning. Then the nine sons, without a thought for their youngest brother, began to spend their money in any way that pleased them. Soon they had spent all of their inheritance.

The youngest brother remembered his father's words about his ten friends. And so, after a time, he called on each of the friends and said, "Before my father died, he asked me to keep you as friends, and I want to honor my promise to him. I am about to leave this place to seek my fortune elsewhere. But before I leave, I would like to invite you to a farewell dinner. Please come so that you may help me keep my word to my father." The friends all accepted this invitation with great pleasure.

At the dinner, the friends engaged in lively conversations, each one in turn remembering a story about their friend, the young man's father. At the end of the modest dinner, one of the friends stood up and said: "Dear friends, we are all recalling our old friend with such great love. And of all his sons, only his youngest has kept his memory alive by remembering his friends. Why should we also not respect our friend and honor him by helping his son? Why should this loyal young man have to go far away from our community to

> According to the sages, six things existed before the creation; one of those was the Torah. The Torah was created by God in the very beginning and served as a guide for the rest of creation but was not given to the children of Israel for twenty-six generations. *(Genesis Rabbah 1.4)*

be with strangers in order to earn a living? Let us each contribute a generous sum of gold and help him establish a business here in our midst."

All the other friends agreed heartily, as they poured glasses of wine for everyone and drank a *l'chaim*, a toast to life.

The young man became a prosperous merchant and always treasured these friends as his own, often remembering his father's words, "My friends will be your companions, and they are worth more than gold and silver."

This is what he taught his own children, and his name, too, was honored through the generations. *(Peninnah Schram)**

*Originally published as "The Ten Sons" in *Jewish Stories One Generation Tells Another,* by Peninnah Schram.

Four Sayings to Live By

God has a special concern for the poor and shows favor toward those who share that concern.

The Story

A good name is more to be desired than great riches; esteem is better than silver or gold. Rich and poor have this in common: the LORD made them both.

. . . .

Whoever sows injustice will reap trouble; the rod of God's wrath will destroy him. One who is kindly will be blessed, for he shares his food with the poor.

. . . .

Never rob anyone who is helpless because he is helpless, nor ill-treat a poor wretch in court; for the LORD will take up their cause and rob of life those who rob them.

Comments on the Story

The Nature of Proverbial Sayings: Unlike the long segments of poetry in Proverbs 1–9, in which themes and images are related by repetition and contrast, the collections of Proverbs contain short, discrete sayings that can be read and savored individually. These sayings, the *meshalim,* or proverbs, give the book its name. The meaning of the Hebrew name for a single saying, *mashal,* cannot be rendered by a single English term. The root of the word means "likeness" or "resemblance." The book of Proverbs is dominated by these sayings, which, strung together in the major collections, constitute the primary literary output of the sages. Tradition has it that Solomon is the author of the book of Proverbs, based on the reference in 1 Kings 4:29-34 NRSV: "He composed three thousand proverbs, and his songs numbered a thousand and five." Proverbs itself contradicts such an assumption, including collections by other authors. While hardly the author of each proverb or poem in the book, Solomon was clearly thought of as the patron saint of the wisdom movement, a status that took its cue from Solomon's politically successful reign.

The proverbs in chapter 22 are found in the second major section in the book of Proverbs (chaps. 10–22:16). In general, this section is characterized by prudential sayings, which advocate right conduct, interspersed with shrewd observations about human behavior. The truth of each saying is to be tested by experience. One could imagine exceptions to every one of these sayings, and in some cases they appear downright naive, especially by today's standards of cleverness. But the sayings are presented as trustworthy because they are fundamentally on the mark. To get the full effect of their power, it helps to read them quickly, taking each as a particular facet of reality and noting the points of repetition as an indication of emphasis in the collection. Together they form a view of the world that corresponded to the sages' vision of human community at its broadest, ranging from what qualified as basic decent behavior to the subtlest exercise of ethical sensitivity.

The core meaning of *mashal* is "comparison" or "likeness." These comparisons take many different literary forms from popular sayings to taunts, and even include persons or events; in the mashal, the idea of comparison counts, not the exact form of its literary structure. Even so, it is thought that the popular proverb is the earliest variety of the *mashal*. The purpose of this kind of *mashal* is simply to register a perceptive observation that may be quoted to give meaning or serve as a guide for future action, such as 1 Samuel 10:12 ("Therefore it became a proverb, 'Is Saul also among the prophets?' ") or 1 Samuel 24:13 NRSV ("As the ancient proverb says, 'Out of the wicked comes forth wickedness' "). The professional class of wise men and women composed proverbs because they recognized that the intellectual and emotional appeal of metaphor could drive home their ethical points. In Proverbs 22:1-2, 8-9, 22-23 we have proverbs in their most refined and polished form, to be used independently as principles for righteous, prosperous, and satisfying living. In addition, verses 22-23 are taken from a subsection within the collection, 22:17–24:22, which is closely modeled on the Egyptian wisdom of Amenemopet.

The first *mashal* we have seen before, when Wisdom claimed her own worth to exceed all the riches of the earth. But here it is not wisdom but a good name and esteem that is worth more than great wealth. (Compare 10:7; Eccles. 7:1; Ecclus. 41:12-13.) The Hebrew word translated "esteem" is ambiguous. The Hebrew root means to show favor or to be gracious in the sense of being merciful and generous, showing consideration. One either offers mercy to others or finds it oneself; and the word *hen* is used chiefly in the latter sense, to find favor with someone, whether it is other people or God.

It is important to note that this saying is meant to be taken at face value. Its truth is deceptively simple. The sage begins with the comparison between public esteem (a good name) and great wealth. A good reputation now has a value placed on it; it is at least as valuable as a fortune, which everybody wants either to get or to keep. But the truth is, according to the sage, that the good reputation has more value than the fortune. Wealth often confers on its possessors the appearance of great probity; the view up close may be far different. A truly good reputation is built on consistant ethical behavior. But even the fortune of a good reputation must be protected against those who delight in

51

maligning others. Shakespeare's villian Iago, a master at inuendo and subversion, knows full well the worth of the reputations he destroys: "Good name in man and woman . . . is the immediate jewel of their souls. Who steals my purse steals trash . . . but he who filches from me my good name robs me of that which not enriches him and makes me poor indeed" *(Othello,* III.3.155-161). For now, however, we have simply the observation that one should value one's good reputation as one would a large fortune; the truth of this proverb is the foundation of a good many subtle variations on the theme of public morality.

In a society in which relative levels of wealth and status divide persons so much that their lives seem totally distinct, with no resemblance whatsoever, the next proverb is a daring statement. The rich can usually find a way to keep the destitute out of their line of vision in their neighborhoods, at their clubs, and in their churches. The poor, with their limited opportunities, may spend their lives within a small radius of space as well. But they meet in one thing: their common humanity, created by God. Once again, the statement seems straightforward enough. But in what does their common humanity consist, and is it enough to make an impact on social and political structures that reinforce the separation between rich and poor?

The background to this proverb is the sages' almost programmatic belief in a system of retribution wherein God rewards the rightous with wealth and the wicked with poverty. This view, which finds clear expression in Psalm 37, for example, suggested that God somehow sponsored a class system based on relative wealth. It also blunted the obligation of the rich to assist the poor.

The collection itself shows a more complex view of what really goes on in human communities. On the one hand, idleness leads inexorably to poverty ("Idle hands make for penury; diligent hands make for riches" [10:4]) and wealth could be honestly possessed ("Their wealth is the crown of the wise, folly the chief ornament of the stupid" [14:24]). But on the other hand, the rich were not to rely on their wealth (11:4, 28) and modest means with peace and harmony were much better than wealth and strife (15:16, 17). Poor people must endure friendlessness (14:20; 19:4, 6-7) and oppression (13:23), even though they are not vulnerable to blackmail (13:8).

Although it appears that the poor have nothing, they have the most powerful ally: their Creator. The abuse of the poor, therefore, is not as inconsequential as it may appear, and once again the wise seek the foundations of human community. It is simply indecent to oppress (14:31), sneer at (17:5), or withhold charity from the poor, as well as to despise the hungry (14:21). It is easy to do and evidently has no cost, but wisdom, which is allied with piety, has no part in it.

So rich and poor are to see the resemblance between themselves in their common origins and nature as created beings. This observation contains the seeds of equitable behavior between rich and poor, but does not offer a prescription for how to achieve it. The wise, it seems to imply, will ponder this reality and devise their own worthy conduct around it.

The final proverb in this series extends the notion of God's special protection of the poor with a threat. Anyone who exploits the weakness of a person for his or her own gain, whether to rob or cheat of justice, will pay for it. This proverb is part of a section that has been modeled on the Egyptian collection the *Sayings of Amenemopet,* which was discovered by archaeologists in the 1920s and is dated to the first half of the first millennium before the common era. Following the instructional form, the sayings in this section are somewhat longer than those surrounding it, befitting the purposes of professional teachers both in Egypt and, later, in Israel. It is worth noting that this subsection of proverbs has its own introduction (22:17-21), comparable to the introduction of the book of Proverbs (1:2-7), and that this proverb is the first in the list of thirty.

This saying shows the clear influence of religious thinking in Egyptian wisdom thought. Indeed, Egyptians held wisdom in special honor, venerating a goddess, Ma'at, as the embodiment of the primordial principle of order in the cosmos, the social principles of righteousness and justice, and the personal virtue of truthfulness that must follow from her existence. In Egyptian religious thought, God is the one who gave right order and who maintains it through his power. Israel's appropriation of Egyptian instructional wisdom in this passage accounts for the strong element of retributive thinking in this proverb. Egypt and Israel shared the idea that one not only ought to be pious and worshipful toward God, but also that one should expect recompense from God for misdeeds that may otherwise go unpunished. Here it is the power of God to make fate deliver what amounts to "poetic justice" that is highlighted.

Behind this is the world view of courtiers associated with the royal school. In Egyptian thought, the youth who was being trained for a life at court was to devote his life to God and Pharaoh, who were all but identified in that great empire. Israel, on the other hand, clearly distinguished king from deity, making the king responsible to Yahweh for the administration of the realm and the enforcement of justice (see 1 Kings 8, for example). But in this Israelite adaptation of Egyptian instruction, the king is not subject to criticism by one who serves him at court. For the young courtier to be instructed by the sage in how to properly stand before the king is the ultimate good and is far superior to developing upper-class pretensions by merely associating with nobles (Prov. 23:1-3, 24:21-24).

But, most important, the upper class youth shall not dishonor himself with highhanded behavior toward those who are at a tremendous disadvantage to him. The Hebrew word *dal* means "poor," but the root meaning of the word suggests more than economic disadvantage alone. There is the overtone of active suffering here, of being brought low and languishing in a diminished state. The *dal* is a social dependent. So if instead of accepting one's role as the protector of the weak and unfortunate (see Job 31), one pushes them closer to death with acts of careless oppression, one will thus understand that God seeks justice against him or her. They have disturbed the divinely ordained pattern of justice in the universe and now—in an entirely fitting way—their own lives are at stake. This is the wisdom equivalent of the famous *lex talionis* in the Israelite law codes: Where injury results from lawbreaking, you shall give an eye for an eye, a tooth for a tooth, a hand for hand, and so forth. For the sage, equal justice is guaranteed by God over the course of a human life.

Retelling the Story

A good name . . . Whoever sows injustice . . . Never rob anyone. (Prov. 22:1, 8, 22)

In Judaism, the rabbis in the Talmud spoke of three crowns: The first is the Crown of Priesthood; the second is the Crown of the Kings; and the third is the Crown of the Good Name *(Shem Tov)*. To obtain the first two crowns, one must be born into the priesthood or the kingly family of David. But the Crown of the Good Name is available to all to acquire and is greater than the others.

There once was a king who knew that he would soon die. He summoned his children and all who were in the palace to come to him, and he said: "Know that I will soon die and I want to bequeath to you your legacy, the way to live so that all may continue to prosper.

When someone meets a poor person who asks for help and thinks, "Why don't you get a job? After all, you have legs to walk and arms to lift, shoulders to carry and a head to think," God responds, "Not only did you not give this poor soul anything, but you have the nerve to complain about what I gave him." (Leviticus Rabbah, 34.7)

Listen well, my children, my builders, my friends. Join together to help one another. Let the less powerful one among you obey the one with greater power, but the greater one shows mercy to all others. Let the one who has knowledge teach the ignorant, and let the ignorant accept the knowledge and learn. Let the wealthy one give to the hungry and poor, and let the needy thank the wealthy. Let the sinner confess his crimes and let

The saying that God made both rich and poor was viewed as a warning to the wealthy by some rabbis. When someone came asking for help, they contended, those who had money should remember this bit of wisdom, since the same God who made them rich could make them poor. On the other hand, that same God could enrich the poor so that their role would be reversed someday. *(Sefer Ha-Aggadah, 669.279)* the one who was done the injustice pardon and accept atonement. Remember that if you live united, you will continue to live in a good way, but if you are divided, you will surely perish."

Then the king turned to his knight and gave him these instructions: "Take ten arrows and try to break the bundle of arrows." The knight used all his strength to try to accomplish what the king had asked of him, but no matter how hard he tried to break these arrows, he could not break them.

Then the king said, "Fling the arrows to the ground." The knight threw the arrows so that they scattered everywhere.

How can one rob another who has nothing, the rabbis asked? Not to rob those who are poor (or helpless) means that those who have enough must offer to the poor the alms that God requires. In ancient times that would include allowing them to glean the fields and the tithe to help support orphans, widows, and aliens. To refuse to give to those in need is to rob the poor and helpless. *(Sefer Ha-Aggadah, 670.282)*

The king called to the youngest attendant and said, "Pick up these arrows one by one and break them." And the attendant, small as he was, snapped each arrow in half, easily.

The same warning concerning robbing the poor and helpless applies to judges, according to certain rabbis. They say that if a judge acts unjustly by finding for one party in a dispute, then that judge is robbing the poor and God will take his life in repayment for his injustice. *(Sefer Ha-Aggadah, 735.140)*

"And so you see," said the king, "how each arrow can be broken when it is separate, but not when they are united. So too will you live and prosper as a community when you help each other, share your wealth, and live with justice." *(Peninnah Schram)*

---

*The source of this tale is Mishle Arav in *Ha-Levanon II* and a version can be found in *Mimekor Yisrael.*

Advice from a Courtier on Humility

The wise do not seek places of honor for themselves.

The Story

Do not push yourself forward at court or take your stand where the great assemble; for it is better to be told, "Come up here," than to be moved down to make room for a nobleman.

Comments on the Story

This brief instruction, which makes clear reference to its background in the royal court, is but one echo of a thought running through the entire Hebrew Bible (and indeed most of the world's religious traditions): the concept of humility. This proverb expresses the ideal as it was enjoined by the sages to their young charges, who were being prepared to take their places in the royal court. The young would-be courtier, who will exercise great responsibility in the nation and who will undoubtedly wield great power in his position, must learn not to promote himself to the company of the wise or great or presume that he is their equal. He must instead be invited on the basis of his virtues as perceived by his superiors. He is not to be "wise in [his] own eyes" (26:12 NRSV) like the scoffer. This behavior earns the Lord's contempt (6:16-17).

For the sage, humility does two things. First, it protects the purity of wisdom, for the student must practice it for its own sake and not simply as a means to something else. But second, the path of humility, of not claiming advantage for oneself, is ultimately the path of success because it allows wisdom to function to its fullest extent, which merits honor. The wise man or woman who is not proud, arrogant, or haughty (see Prov. 13:10; 11:2; 16:18; 18:12) can be successful because he or she defines success in its fullest sense of being in one's proper place in the universe, at peace with both God and humankind. This measure of success eschews the crude desire for either fame or fortune alone. The wise individual alone is worthy of honor (29:23), which others will certainly accord ("Let another praise you, and not your own mouth" [27:2 NRSV]). Riches may indeed follow such genuine acclaim; the sages see no evil in that. But prosperity in itself is not the goal, only an accoutrement of a life well lived.

The sage advocated humility because he was aware that even wisdom was subject to God: "Face to face with the LORD, wisdom, understanding, counsel avail nothing" (21:30). God provides the limits of wisdom, both at its points of origin ("The fear of the LORD is the foundation of knowledge" [1:7]) and at its end, when wisdom must give way to divine authority. Sirach will spell out this theme distinctly:

> My son, in all you do be unassuming,
> and those whom the Lord approves will love you.
> The greater you are, the humbler must you be,
> and the Lord will show you favour.
> for his power is great,
> yet he reveals his secrets to the humble.
> . . . .
> Meditate on what the Lord has commanded;
> what he has kept hidden need not concern you.
> (Ecclus. 3:17-20, 22)

So humility, which alone lets men and women recognize their true place in the universe, lies at the heart of wisdom ethics.

But the proverb itself gives no hint of such theological verities. It merely states that the wise man does not manifest his ambition in public; if he waits, he will be invited, saving himself the embarrassment of being removed from his place to make room for a grandee who is perceived to be his better.

In the New Testament, this sentiment is used both by Jesus and about him. In the first instance, in Luke 14:7-11, Jesus notices guests making efforts to secure for themselves the seats of honor at a banquet. He makes a comparison (in Luke it is called a parable) between places of honor at a banquet and the eschatological banquet that is to come: "For everyone who exalts himself will be humbled; and whoever humbles himself will be exalted." About Jesus it was sung in the earliest Christian communities: "He was in the form of God; yet he laid no claim to equality with God, but made himself nothing, assuming the form of a slave. Bearing the human likeness, sharing the human lot, he humbled himself, and was obedient, even to the point of death, death on a cross! Therefore God raised him" (Phil. 2:6-9).

Retelling the Story

Do not push yourself forward at court. (Prov. 25:6)

Just as instructions on how to treat people wisely are given throughout the book of Proverbs, so, too, good advice is given in this folktale to the rabbinical students as they are about to leave their school and take on responsibilities as leaders in their communities.

The young rabbi had completed his studies and was ready to leave the academy. He was ready to return home, his heart filled with hope. And he had a new title, which he had earned with the highest honors. He felt the pride of accomplishment—and why not? For years, had he not worked hard, studying, learning, questioning, attaining the admiration and the highest rank among his companions? And now it was time to bid farewell to his friends and to the head of the academy.

The head of the academy addressed all the students before they left: "My students, or rather I should say, my masters, for all these years I have learned most from you, my devoted students, what advice can I give you as you leave the academy? You have great knowledge, strong ambition, and you have gained my sincere respect. Yours is a holy purpose that you must not abuse. Remember always that the responsibilities of a gifted teacher are the most sacred. I will give you this rule to guide you. Let this principle be as an angel guiding you on the way: Be pliant as the reed—that is, be kindly to all; and never be unbending as the cedar—that is, unforgiving to him who insults you. My dear friends, why was the reed chosen to be used as a pen for writing the Torah scroll, the tefillin (phylacteries) and the mezuzot (parchment scroll with the name of God attached to the doorposts)? It gained merit because of its special quality. You, too, will gain merit if you remember this principle and apply it."

A rabbi named Jesus of Nazareth told his disciples a story that seems to have direct reference to this passage. He said that when they went to a wedding feast they were not to take the places that had been reserved for the guests of honor. They might be embarrassed when the host came and asked them to make room for someone more important. When they went, he instructed them, they were to take the places with the least prestige so the host might ask them to come to a place of greater honor. Instead of being embarrassed, they would be honored by all in attendance. Then he sums the story up by telling them that those who think highly of themselves will be humbled and those who are lowly will be given positions of honor. (Luke 14:8-11)

After the farewells, the young rabbi began his journey home. As he rode, he could hardly keep from thinking about the reception waiting for him. After all, he was returning with the title of "rabbi," and the town would shower him with honor for his learning as well as for his title. It was a beautiful bright morning and, as he rode, he listened to the birds and enjoyed the flowering meadow, all the time imagining the welcome he would receive. "Master! Master!" a hoarse voice called out, interrupting his daydream.

He turned to see who had

called out, but his mood was one of anger. Who was pulling him out of this wonderful dream, this young rabbi, whom all delighted to honor?

When he looked down, he saw that it was a poor dwarf, crouching in the road. When the dwarf happily saw that he was noticed, he called out again, "Master! Master!"

At that point the young rabbi exclaimed in a scornful tone: "Tell me, have all the townspeople faces as ugly as yours? I would like to know before I continue my journey."

The dwarf was used to contempt, but this time he felt the pain even deeper than ever and he replied, "I do not know. Why not go to the Artist who made me and reproach him for his handiwork? It was not my doing."

Suddenly, quick like an arrow hitting the mark, the rule "pliant as the reed," his rabbi's parting advice, sprang into his mind. And now how had he applied it? Had he been kindly to this poor broken *nefesh* (soul)? What good was all his learning compared with the dignity of a human soul that he had treated with such contempt? Overwhelmed by a sudden sense of worthlessness, the young rabbi went over to the dwarf and threw himself to the ground and exclaimed, "Forgive me for my rudeness! I was hasty in my reply. I have sinned against you, but I ask for your forgiveness!"

The dwarf did not so easily accept this apology. Words that have stung cannot be taken back so quickly. The dwarf made only one reply. "Go reproach the Artist for his work! Perhaps you consider yourself a better artist!"

They continued walking to the town, and what a strange pair they were, with the dwarf walking first, followed by the rabbi, half pleading and half reasoning with the dwarf. But the dwarf would not be comforted. And all this caused the rabbi to lose his golden dreams. The very landscape had changed. The sun no longer seemed to shine as brightly. The birds were no longer singing. Everyone in the village knew that the young rabbi, who had left years before as a child, was returning. There was great excitement in the town because the people there had always regarded a religious teacher with great esteem. And to have their own rabbi, born in that very town, and such a rabbi of learning and reputation, gave them an even greater *koved* (honor) indeed. There was joy and anticipation.

Knowing that this was the day of his arrival, the people gathered and started walking down the road to meet the young rabbi even before he would reach the town. Seeing him in the distance, they ran toward him, shouting, *"Sholom aleikhem,* O master! Peace be unto you, O teacher!" The young rabbi did not know how to respond, as he felt such deep humiliation and self-reproach over what had happened on the road. But the people understood his silence as a sign of his modesty, and their admiration for him increased even more.

All this time, the dwarf mingled with the crowd and heard all the praise lavished on the young rabbi. But after a while the dwarf called out, "Who are you honoring in this way?"

"What? You don't know that this is our new rabbi, a scholar and a learned teacher? One of our own?"

"Scholar! Rabbi! Learned teacher! Keep us from such teachers! Listen, people, and judge between me and your rabbi." And the dwarf told them of the insult he had received. Everyone listened in silence, and one look at the young rabbi's face confirmed that what the dwarf was saying was what had happened. The people saw his anguish and his sorrow.

And then the young rabbi spoke, and his words came from a wound in his heart. "I have wronged this man. It was a shameful, cruel action, and I am truly sorry for my foolish words. I confess it openly. What more can I do? I have asked him to forgive me, but he is as unbending as the cedar. I had hoped to come to you with joy, but my soul is filled with sorrow and grief."

This same Jesus of Nazareth went on to teach his disciples that when they gave a party they were not to invite their friends or relatives or wealthy neighbors. Rather, they were to invite those who are blind, those who cannot walk, and the poor. In this way they will have invited those who could never repay their invitation, and their reward will be in God's hands. (Luke 14:12-14)

"Pardon him! Pardon him!" cried out the people. "Pardon him for his wisdom's sake. Look in his eyes and you can see his true repentance."

"Yes, I shall pardon him," replied the dwarf after a silence. "I shall pardon him for your sakes and that he may never commit again so grievous a sin." And when the young rabbi lifted his face to thank the dwarf for his forgiveness, the dwarf was nowhere to be seen.

"Perhaps the dwarf was Elijah the Prophet," he wondered. And for the first time since the morning, he had a smile on his face and the sorrow in his heart had lifted.

The next day was Shabbat. The young rabbi was to preach his first sermon, so people came from everywhere to hear him. The young rabbi did not feel any fear, but rather a new kind of excitement. After all, he had learned more from one day's experience than from years of study and thought. He had felt humility and compassion in a way in which he had never understood these feelings before. He realized that it was a valuable lesson and that more could be learned from studying people than from studying only books. He felt a new sense of gratitude and joy. Wrestling with these thoughts, the young rabbi got up from his chair and approached the pulpit to begin his sermon. People grew quiet, and everyone's attention was on the rabbi.

The rabbi began to speak: "Be always pliant as the reed, and never be unbending as the cedar." *(Peninnah Schram)*

*Originally published as "The Repentant Rabbi" in *Tales of Elijah the Prophet* by Peninnah Schram.

A Woman of Substance

The wise woman keeps both household and business going and is praised for all her many gifts.

The Story

Who can find a good wife?
  Her worth is far beyond red
  coral.
Her husband's whole trust is in her,
  and children are not lacking.
She works to bring him good, not evil,
  all the days of her life.
She chooses wool and flax
  and with a will she sets about her
  work.
Like a ship laden with merchandise
  she brings home food from far off.
She rises while it is still dark
  and apportions food for her household,
with a due share for her servants.
After careful thought she buys a field
  and plants a vineyard out of her
  earnings.
She sets about her duties resolutely
  and tackles her work with vigour.
She sees that her business goes well,
  and all night long her lamp does not
  go out.
She holds the distaff in her hand,
  and her fingers grasp the spindle.
She is open-handed to the wretched
  and extends help to the poor.
When it snows she has no fear for her
  household,
  for they are wrapped in double
  cloaks.

She makes her own bed coverings
  and clothing of fine linen and purple.
Her husband is well known in the
  assembly,
  where he takes his seat with the
  elders of the region.
She weaves linen and sells it,
  and supplies merchants with sashes.
She is clothed in strength and dignity
  and can afford to laugh at tomorrow.
When she opens her mouth, it is to
  speak wisely;
  her teaching is sound.
She keeps her eye on the conduct of
  her household
  and does not eat the bread of idleness.
Her sons with one accord extol her
  virtues;
  her husband too is loud in her
  praise:
"Many a woman shows how gifted she
  is;
  but you excel them all."
Charm is deceptive and beauty fleeting;
  but the woman who fears the LORD is
  honoured.
Praise her for all she has accomplished;
  let her achievements bring her hon-
  our at the city gates.

Comments on the Story

In the Hebrew Bible, the endings of books or multi-volume works are never a matter of indifference. In the end of Genesis, for example, the patriarch Joseph has died at a ripe old age and is laid in a coffin in Egypt. His death is the symbolic bridge between the families of Jacob and the new people of Israel, who will leave Egypt under Moses. The end of Judges, a chronicle of death and destruction, is marked by the quiet comment, "In those days there was no king in Israel; everyone did what was right in his own eyes" (21:25). This raises our expectation that Proverbs 31:10-31 might offer a heightened sense of an ending to the entire collection.

The sages' decision to end Proverbs with a poem in praise of a worthy woman will disappoint some. But the poem praising a worthy woman weaves many conceptual strands from the preceding chapters together into a concrete, but idealized, form. For here is what can become of the "wife of one's youth" if she herself pursues the path of wisdom as he does. Many commentators have noted that this worthy woman provides an example for a young Israelite to emulate. But instead of seeing it as an ancient text for Mother's Day, we will understand the poem far better if we do not avoid the male context that both Lady Wisdom and the Israelite educational environment presume.

In the ancient world, two factors united to prevent women from assuming prominent roles in society: the sheer amount of labor for which women were accountable, and the lack of literacy in general. Women had full responsibility for maintaining the household. Domestic life, then as now, was filled with end-less routine. But it also required informal knowledge of numerous topics, such as herbal lore, weaving and dying, shopping and maintaining household stores, supervising servants, and so forth. The fewer servants, the more backbreaking labor of cooking and cleaning fell directly on the wife (in an extended family, these tasks could be delegated to female family members). Training in these responsibilities began early for girls, who were prepared by their mothers to assume this role in their own homes. Boys, on the other hand, were separated from their mothers for their education, the crown of which was learning to read and write. But these skills were specialized and not all, presumably, received instruction at this level. Literacy rates in ancient Egypt have been estimated no more than 1 percent of the population. It would have been well nigh impossible for a girl to excel in both domains. Still, there are examples of women who were trained as scribes in Mesopotamia and Egypt (although their skills were employed for other women, princesses and royal harems, where male contact was deliberately restricted).

Women, therefore, were tied to their families, whether the family into which they were born or the one into which they married. But their true esteem in their families was linked to the performance of their expected duties and, necessarily, their moral qualities. The woman who managed a household was accounted as wise in the ancient world, and this honor is reflected in the adjective applied to her: *worthy*. The Hebrew word *hayil* means "strong" or "valiant" and is usually applied to warriors. The total competence displayed by the worthy woman may even be reflected in the form of the poem, the acrostic, in which each line begins with a letter of the alphabet, from *aleph* to *taw*. This social reality is the basis for the praise of woman in Proverbs 31:10-31.

But more than this, the worthy woman is touched with the dignity and authority of Lady Wisdom. Like wisdom, the worthy woman is more precious than jewels to her husband. Having her, he is assured of goodness in life. Her industry, like that of Lady Wisdom, builds up the household for him. Like Lady Wisdom, she creates and inhabits a mental and moral universe in which he has a necessary part. Living in this environment and joining in her praise, he manifests his own love of wisdom. Extolling her virtues publicly raises his own status in the assembly of men at the city gate.

The question remains whether this passage is effective as a role model for young women, whether in ancient times or today. There are difficulties with this: Few women have the opportunity to actually run a large household as this upper-class woman does. Women who take on less conventional responsibilities are ignored in the biblical text. But the crucial problem is that this poem does not describe for women the quest for wisdom that animates the educational goals of the book of Proverbs as a whole. The worthy woman is presented to us as a paragon of virtue, as a goddess. The woman's story, her evolution as a wise person, is not here. To present the fruit of the struggle without the narrative behind it does not empower.

In the end, therefore, this passage is less useful for women than it is for men. And here its meaning blossoms freely. Proverbs 31:10-31 is meant to convey to them the full significance of the well-run household and the person who is at its core. When he sees the resemblance between his wife and the Lady Wisdom who guides and blesses his whole life, the home is furnished with new meaning. It mirrors his own labor in the world, his own drive for recognition and respect among his peers, his own quest for depth and insight. Seen in this light, the worthy woman is indeed a powerful *mashal*—an emblem to teach and guide future generations.

Retelling the Story

Who can find a good wife? (Prov. 31:10)

There once were three friends who after a day's work would meet on the porch of the coffeehouse to talk. They often talked about what they wished to have in their lives, for in truth they all had very little. One evening, the first

This extraordinary tribute to a "virtuous woman," an *eshet chayil,* is recited traditionally by husbands to their wives at the beginning of the Friday evening meal, which ushers in the Sabbath. The same phrase can be found in Proverbs 12:4 and also applied to Ruth, in the book of Ruth, when Boaz says to her, "For all the men in the gate of my people do know that thou art a virtuous woman" (Ruth 3:11). It is interesting to note that the "Hebrew" [of the opening line] is incorrectly construed as a question, as though the writer's intention was 'a good wife is not easily found, but when she is found, she is of inestimable value.' The sense is: whoever has married such a woman knows from his experience how priceless is her worth." (A. Cohen, *Proverbs* [London: The Soncino Press, 1967], Ft. 10, p. 211)

man said, "If only I had money, I would perform *mitzvot* (good deeds) and help the poor."

The second friend said, "If only I had wisdom, I would build schools, especially so the poor children could learn."

Then the third friend spoke. "If only I could find a good woman, an *eshet chayil,* I would marry her."

That evening, Elijah the Prophet, in the disguise of a jester, happened to be walking by. He stopped and ordered some coffee and listened. Then he turned to the three young men and asked, "Are you speaking the truth? Would you give to the poor if they came to your door? Would you really practice what you say?"

"Of course," answered the first friend.

Elijah took one coin from his purse and gave it to the young man. "Take this coin on condition that you will use it wisely to help and sustain those in need."

Then he turned to the second young man and asked, "Would you really do what you say, build schools, especially to educate the poor children?"

"Yes, I would," replied the second friend.

Elijah took a page from a book that lined his cap and gave it to the second young man. "Take this page and with it learn all you can while you build schools for the poor children, as you promised."

Now turning to the third friend, Elijah asked, "And would you marry a good woman if you found her?"

"Gladly I would do that," answered the third friend.

"In that case," said Elijah, "ask the young woman who lives next door to marry you."

The following morning, the first friend woke up and found that he was rich, very rich! Remembering his promise, he began to distribute money for charity everywhere. He helped people who came to him for money. He gave charity

Beauty is fleeting, say the rabbis. In fact, there were six students of one rabbi who believed this so deeply that they made do with one coat among them so they could have time to study Torah. Perhaps they learned the wisdom of sharing at the same time. *(Sefer Ha-Aggadah 256.256)*

wherever he traveled. But after a few years, he became tired of performing these good deeds and stopped. Instead, he kept all his money for himself.

The second friend woke up and found that he could easily learn whatever he wanted to know. He built a few schools, but he began to accept only rich families' children. Finally, when there was no room in the schools for any additional children, he stopped.

The third young man had met his neighbor's daughter. She always appeared bad-tempered, but, he thought, why not? At least it was convenient to court her. And so they were married.

After several years had passed, Elijah decided to test these three young men to see how they were faring. In the disguise of a traveler, Elijah came to the mansion of the first friend. When the servant came to the door, he asked to see the master. After waiting a long time, the master himself came to the door and the traveler asked to spend the holiday with him.

"Servant, give this poor traveler a coin from the pile," was the master's reply, spoken in a brusque voice.

"In that case," said Elijah, "give me the original coin I gave to you years ago."

"What's the difference? One coin looks like any other—there's no difference. Who are you, anyway? A jester?" asked the master in a mocking tone.

"Exactly," answered Elijah. "Open your drawer and there you will find the original coin. Return it to me."

The master obeyed and returned the original coin to Elijah. As Elijah disappeared around the bend of the road, the mansion suddenly became a small cottage and the servants began beating the formerly rich man, demanding their wages.

Elijah, in the disguise of an old man, then went to the second friend. He had with him a poor child to register in the school. When the friend came to the door and saw the poor child, he called out, "We have no room here. I am fed up with accepting poor children who cannot pay."

"Well then, give me back my original page. You will find it under your pillow," ordered Elijah.

"Are you crazy, old man? How will I find a page after so many years, especially under a pillow? You surely are jesting," the second friend said with a laugh.

"I never jest," answered Elijah. "Give back that original page. It is under your pillow," he repeated.

The second friend lifted his pillow and found the page and returned it to Elijah. Suddenly black smoke poured from the building as the children all ran from the school to safety. And Elijah disappeared.

Meanwhile, Elijah, in the disguise of a poor man, came to the small cottage of the third friend. The wife was home, and when she saw a poor, hungry person, she invited him to wash before anything else. "I'm dirty and my clothes are ragged," said Elijah.

"No matter," answered the wife. "Here are some of my husband's clothing. They will fit you. My husband is at work but soon he will return home." And while Elijah washed and changed his clothes, the wife prepared some food. After eating, she led the poor man to the bedroom to rest. She closed the door and waited outside for her husband because she did not want to disturb the guest's sleep—and also out of modesty.

When finally her husband returned, she went toward him to greet him. She told him about their guest. "And husband, do not be angry with me for I gave him the food I had prepared for our supper."

"Dear wife, thank goodness I married you. I now see that although you first appeared to be ill-tempered, you are a good woman who performs good deeds that save us from hard times," answered the husband.

The sages say that the righteous do not work for rewards or honor in this life but for the good that is prepared for them in the world to come. When Rabbi Abbahu faced death he was heard to laugh and say, "All of this is for Abbahu." The rabbis say he had simply gotten a glimpse of what was in store for him in the world to come. *(Exodus Rabbah 52.3)*

Elijah heard all of this and said to them, "I give you and your children wealth and learning, because of your good wife's deeds. In your home, you will know how to use the wealth wisely and to help others, and you will know how to share your knowledge and learning only for good and not for evil." And Elijah gave them the coin and the page. Before he left, he blessed them, saying, "May you see many blessed days until the end."

And so may we all! *(Peninnah Schram)*

*Originally published as "Elijah's Three Gifts" in *Tales of Elijah the Prophet* by Peninnah Schram. This story is from a medieval collection, *Sefer Ha-Mussar,* and variants can be found in the Jewish European folktales as well as in the *Israel Folktale Archives* from Morocco, Iraq, and Tunisia. Another version is in Schram's *Jewish Stories One Generation Tells Another.*

II. Job:

A Narrative Introduction

The book of Job is unique in the Israelite wisdom literature because the main character was already known in biblical times as a hero of righteousness and intercessory prayer (Ezek. 14:12-20). Like Noah and Daniel, the other legendary figures cited by the prophet, Job was a byword among the Jewish exiles in Babylon. The mention of his name evoked the remembrance of his story: a righteous, wealthy man whom God tested first by depriving him of everything short of his life and then by restoring it again. The idea of the byword finds an echo in the book, where Job calls himself a "byword" *(mashal)* whom God has cursed (17:6). The word *mashal* applies to the book of Job in two ways: its main character is not a historical figure but an emblem, a "fiction" as the rabbis later saw it, representing the righteous sufferer. In addition, the book of Job as a whole can be seen as a wisdom parable.

Anyone reading the book of Job today inherits the biblical perception that Job—the character and the book—is a parable. But a parable about what? By the Common Era, Job was thought to be a *mashal* about patience (James 5:10-11), and this is still a popular way to simplify the book based on a reading of the first two chapters. But the book of Job is about patience (or the lack of it) as much as Melville's great novel *Moby Dick* is about a whale. The book of Job carries scriptural authority, of course, but it is also a classic of world literature. As in any complex work of art, there are worlds of meaning to explore before we arrive at the place where a simple, existential statement about the meaning of Job carries weight.

We can begin to approach Job by noting that its basic theme, the problem of innocent suffering, has been treated in two distinct ways in both ancient and modern times. One way is systematic and philosophical, addressing the problem of justifying God's goodness, given the existence of evil (theodicy, Gr. *theos* ["God"] and *dike* ["righteousness"]). Classical Greek philosophers, whose rational view of the cosmos never adequately accounted for the origins of evil or unmerited human suffering, left a challenge for European philosophers. For example, the eighteenth-century English philosopher David Hume wrote a treatise on this question in the form of a dispute. One of the characters summarizes the problem neatly: "Why is there any misery at all in the world?

Not by chance, surely. From some cause then. Is it from the intention of the Deity? But he is perfectly benevolent. Is it contrary to his intention? But he is almighty" (*Dialogues Concerning Natural Religion*, X). The crux of the matter can be expressed in a short saying: If God is God, he is not good; if God is good, he is not God. In the fact of evil, God's absolute goodness will always be pitted against God's absolute power. Evil necessitates a compromise of one or the other.

The question of innocent suffering has also been explored through poetry and drama. Ancient poets in Mesopotamia and Egypt explored the problem of unmerited suffering in a number of works, most of which culminated in the reaffirmation of piety and humility before the gods, regardless of its cost in human pain and suffering. A few, however, reached more daring conclusions: In the Babylonian Theodicy (c.1000 B.C.E.) suffering is blamed on the gods, who made humankind evil and, therefore, caused misfortune and oppression on earth. An Egyptian poem, "A Dispute Over Suicide," reviews the situation and recommends death as the final human triumph over pain. The closest analogy to the book of Job in this literature is found in a work entitled "Ludlul bel nemeqi," or "I Will Praise the Lord of Wisdom," which has been called the "Babylonian Job" (c.1500 B.C.E.). The hero of the story is afflicted with a terrible disease and realizes that his divine protection has abandoned him. He endures physical and emotional torment for a year, and in the end has three dreams in which spiritual beings offer sacrifice to the gods for him. This appeases the deity, and the sufferer is restored.

The Greek playwright Aeschylus also treated the problem of unmerited suffering in *Prometheus Bound,* which exposes the heartlessness of the ancient Greek anthropomorphic deities. The story of Job has inspired several poets and playwrights in modern times, including Robert Frost and Archibald MacLeish. Scholars have pointed out that the plot of Job is actually comedic, since it begins with peace and prosperity and descends through great trauma but is ultimately resolved happily.

This parallel literature raises questions that may help us to frame our initial reactions to the book of Job. The philosophical works on the problem of evil direct our attention to God's character as it is manifested in his relationship with the Adversary and his treatment of Job. The poetic and dramatic presentations of the story of innocent suffering remind us that Job must choose between submission to God or rebellion against him; they also highlight the role of debate between friends for bringing the meaning of pain and suffering to light. Is the tension created by Job's affliction resolved in the end, or are significant problems allowed to stand without resolution?

To find answers to these questions, the reader must become familiar with the structure of the book and its particular way of stating truths. This is no easy task. The book has a complex shape, beginning and ending with a prose narrative (sometimes called a folktale) that sets forth the circumstances of the plot and defines the main characters (chaps. 1–2; 42:7-17). In between these sections there is a long poetic dialogue with its own structure, beginning with a soliloquy by Job (chap. 3), followed by three rounds of dispute between Job and the friends who have come to console him; a poem about wisdom (chap. 28); another testimony by Job (chaps. 29–31); a long speech by a new character, the young Elihu (chaps. 32–37); and two speeches by God from the whirlwind plus Job's response (chaps. 38–42:6). The final section returns to prose, as Job's fortunes are restored and he lives "happily ever after."

There is a great temptation to break this complex work down to manageable parts, such as the folktale alone or the poetic dialogue, or even to ignore some passages (the damaged third round of debates or the speeches of Elihu, for example). But the work should be considered as a whole to avoid distorting its message, and there are good reasons to assume that it is the work of a single author.

Although the book may appear overwhelmingly complex, in reality some of its main ideas are shared by each of the characters. Both Job and his three friends, for example, subscribe to the notion of retribution set forth in Proverbs (and Deuteronomy). Each believes that God will not allow the righteous to suffer calamity, but that God is reserving misfortune as a punishment for the wicked sometime in their lifetime. Job's status as the greatest man in the East is due to his righteousness, which is demonstrated by his habit of offering extra sacrifices for his children to cover any "blasphemy in their hearts" (1:5). After God afflicts him, Job does not abandon the principle; instead, he sees clearly that there are many exceptions to the rule, his own case being chief among them (see chaps. 17, 21, 27). As for the friends, they not only affirm the principle, but they also apply it to Job and his children with increasing severity, even alleging that Job has violated his ethical obligations toward the poor, strangers, and widows and orphans (22:6-11), and has thus merited his suffering. In essence, the friends do not believe in innocent victims; where there is misfortune, blame can and must always be assigned.

Job and the three friends also agree on the importance of experience, another central theme in wisdom literature. But once again, this common starting point is quickly abandoned under the pressure of explaining Job's debasement. Job's experience of suffering blots out his belief in a universe ordered by religious practice and the maintenance of social position. Although he has no way to prove it, he correctly accuses God of tormenting him. Because God has shown himself to be an enemy, the world is a hideous place. The order of Job's universe has come undone. Beyond his own misery, he can see only that his friends have betrayed him and that the wicked escape judgment. He will continue to assert his innocence until he is confronted by God from the whirlwind, and he is ultimately vindicated when God declares to the friends that "unlike my servant Job, you have not spoken as you ought about me" (42:7).

The friends also believe in the power of experience. Not having endured suffering comparable to Job's, they must rely on the word from their elders about the meaning of suffering. The friends do not simply counter Job's experience of suffering with cold-blooded, rationalistic theories. Rather, they rely on their own trustworthy experience about the authority of the wisdom tradition, which Job's experiences threaten to undermine. The interaction between Job and the friends has the earmarks of a debate, not a consoling conversation. As their differences become more and more pronounced, Job and his friends grow mean spirited toward one another. It is only their shared experience of God's presence in the end that has a chance of healing the breach between them.

The third point of commonality between Job and his friends (including Elihu) is implicit in the first two. It is of utmost importance to all five of them that their understanding of God's activity in the world be true. There is, in the book of Job, a great deal of theology proper—that is, questions about the nature of God. This is accomplished by several means, including the imitation of psalms of lament and praise and the ancient Israelite covenant piety, with its legal dimension (which was also adapted for use by the eighth-century prophets Micah and Isaiah). The use of the lament by Job in particular testifies to the presence of God in Israelite worship; by aggressively stating his complaint before God, he acknowledges God as the only one with the power both to afflict and to deliver him. In praise, the same thing occurs: Job affirms God as the active source of all that is in the cosmos and among human beings, for better or, in this case, for worse. In adopting the posture of legal and covenantal responsibility toward God, he acknowledges that God is both his accuser and his judge. These dual roles provide much of the emotional pathos in the book. The friends for their part praise God as the defender of cosmic and moral law. They are concerned to protect the power and justice of God against human accusation, limiting access to God in the form of extraordinary mystical experiences. The friends, however, do not lament.

In the end, when God appears in the book of Job, he both confirms and transcends all statements made about him. God appears first to Job but ignores Job's special circumstances completely—and then addresses himself with unprecedented particularity to the friends. He upholds the order of the cosmos and its moral order for humanity (40:11-13), but portrays himself as the creator of Leviathan and Behemoth, who are the true masters of the earth. So Job and the friends are equally correct theologically, but it is clear that such correctness counts for little.

A storyteller following the readings from the Revised Common Lectionary, which are drawn from Job, would highlight portions of the book that have to do chiefly with the relationship between Job and his God. The signal interaction between Job and the friends is telescoped into the opening passage concerning the conflict between Job and his wife. Despite the lack of passages about the friends, there is enough complexity in these readings to suggest the majesty and difficulty of the whole book. The author of Job, probably a master of Israelite wisdom writing for the first generation of intellectuals in the exile, 585–570 B.C.E., produced a religious classic. In his effort to account to his fellow Jews for the destruction of the Temple in Jerusalem and break the pattern of despair and shame they felt over its loss, he composed a parable of innocent suffering and ultimate grace. It is even possible that the book of Job was written to be performed as an actual drama, given the fact that Temple services were no longer being held. So successful was the writer of Job in transmuting the pain of the exiles into an experience of hope that the legendary figure of Job attained mythic status virtually overnight. The "solution" to Israel's exile was a religious vision so potent that the rabbis later wrote: "Had he not raised a cry, even as we now say in the *Tefillah* 'God of Abraham, God of Isaac, and God of Jacob,' we would also be saying 'and God of Job' " *(Pesikta Rabbati* 47:3, ed. M. Friedmann, Yale Judaica Series, vol. XVIII [New Haven: Yale University Press, 1968]).

Job and the Heavenly Wager

God is challenged by a trickster called the Adversary, and a good man named Job suffers.

The Story

There lived in the land of Uz a man of blameless and upright life named Job, who feared God and set his face against wrongdoing. . . .

Once again the day came when the members of the court of heaven took their places in the presence of the LORD, and the Adversary was there among them. The LORD enquired where he had been. 'Ranging over the earth,' said the Adversary, 'from end to end.' The LORD asked, 'Have you considered my servant Job? You will find no one like him on earth, a man of blameless and upright life, who fears God and sets his face against wrongdoing. You incited me to ruin him without cause, but he still holds fast to his integrity.' The Adversary replied, 'Skin for skin! To save himself there is nothing a man will withhold. But just reach out your hand and touch his bones and his flesh, and see if he will not curse you to your face.' The LORD said to the Adversary, 'So be it. He is in your power; only spare his life.'

When the Adversary left the LORD's presence, he afflicted Job with running sores from the soles of his feet to the crown of his head, and Job took a piece of a broken pot to scratch himself as he sat among the ashes. His wife said to him, 'Why do you still hold fast to your integrity? Curse God, and die!' He answered, 'You talk as any impious woman might talk. If we accept good from God, shall we not accept evil?' Throughout all this, Job did not utter one sinful word.

Comments on the Story

As a distillation of the opening narrative of the book of Job, which provides the basic storyline and information about the characters in the book as a whole, this lectionary reading is surprisingly effective. The first two chapters of Job are usually called a folktale, but the simplicity of this story is deceptive. In fact, the writer has constructed a powerful web of meaning in a total of four short scenes, each taking place either in heaven or on earth. The repetition, dialogue between characters, and use of key words are all strategies for intensifying the strain on Job until he breaks the silence with a curse. Building up to this point, not a word is wasted.

The introduction of Job as a character in the chapter (1:1-5) is accomplished in many ways: by his name, his personal qualities, his possessions, and his characteristic activities. The portrait of a patriarch emerges from all these details; like the fathers and mothers of Israel, Job was pious and wealthy, the head of a large household and the leader of the family's religious practice. Job is not an Israelite, and the land of Uz seems deliberately obscure. Of greater apparent significance are Job's personal attributes: integrity and uprightness, piety toward God and morality toward humankind. The words for "integrity" and "uprightness" have an almost visual quality: the Hebrew word for "integrity" *(tam,* from *tumma)* means "completeness" or "wholeness," like a circle. Uprightness has to do with going straight ahead on a path, not deviating to the left or the right, "straight arrow" behavior. This is who Job was; everything he owned (including children) and everything he did regularly were the outward expressions of this status.

The next verse (2:1) takes up the story after two scenes have already occurred, one (1:6-12) in heaven and the other (1:13-22) on earth. The vision of God as a king seated on a throne surrounded by his attendants, the "sons of God" *(bene elohim)* is a familiar one. Similar settings are described in 1 Kings 22:19; Psalms 29:1-2; 82:1; 89:5-8; and Daniel 7:9-10. This image of God stresses his absolute power and control over the cosmos, but it also furnishes a sense of the distance between the deity and humankind. The heavenly realm has its own personnel, hierarchy, and agenda, which runs concurrently with events on earth. Perhaps these dual worlds will intersect—and perhaps they will not. When the distance between them is mediated, things begin to happen for Job.

The distance is first bridged by the all-seeing eye of God, who has noticed the perfection of Job on earth. He boasts about Job to the Adversary *(ha-satan),* an angelic being who crosses between the worlds with a mission: to test and to probe the innermost nature of human beings. Although later tradition made the term *satan* into a proper name and associated him with the origins of evil, this book does not do so. There is nothing particularly menacing about the Adversary, but his job is to express doubt and skepticism. With a lesser man, his doubts would be rewarded with the discovery of human weakness in some form. But Job's excellence has beguiled both God and the Adversary, and the Adversary puts his suspicion up against God's confidence in a wager that Job's piety is rooted in self-interest (1:9, "Has not Job good reason to be godfearing?").

To work out the bet, they agree to test him. In this mutual undertaking they are virtually the same being: God's role is to see, and the Adversary's role is to cross to the other world and destroy. Job, however, knows nothing of this. While we witness the violent end of Job's herds—his total wealth—and his children, Job simply receives the solemn message, delivered four times: "Only I have escaped to bring you the news."

In this first round, which is assumed by our story, God is the winner. Job is able to see that his possessions are all gifts from God that can be taken away at God's pleasure and as a matter of right. In blessing God (1:21), Job declares that God has not violated or exceeded the prerogatives of a deity. Job's piety has survived the tragedy, and this is the basis for the narrator's judgment that Job endured the test and did not sin.

The narrator now returns to the heavenly council for scene three (2:1-6), where our story picks up. On another day of the full assembly, God inquires about the Adversary's whereabouts. He has been ranging (the verb means to walk back and forth) over the earth, doing his job. We now know that God's pride in his servant Job will not rest with quiet satisfaction. When God points out Job to the Adversary, he has in fact initiated another round of testing. Will Job accept physical torment from the hand of God as being within the prerogatives of the deity? Or will he cry foul (i.e., curse God to his face)?

In the fourth and final scene, Job is afflicted with a terrible skin disease, which removes him from active authority in his home to the role of a mourner in the ash heap (the dung heap outside the city is an invention of the Greek translation of the book). Job's wife now makes her first and only appearance. The counsel she offers, to curse God and die, echoes the Adversary, who has predicted that Job will curse God in response to his trials. She uses the word for "bless," not "curse," but here as in a few other instances in the Hebrew Bible its connotations are unmistakable—a blessing overdone, sarcastic, ultimately insincere is in reality a curse. Job's wife has devised a strategy for Job to exert control over his circumstances. She wants him to take the heart out of his blessing and receive the punishment of the wicked for it. In responding to her, Job makes his choice to remain firm in his piety. He accuses her of talking like a fool, and that, as we learn from Proverbs, consists of speaking sharply and without sense (see, for example, Prov. 15:1-4).

Job, on the other hand, does not utter one sinful word. His silence will be broken in chapter 3, when he utters a curse on the day of his birth.

Retelling the Story

"Have you considered my servant Job? You will find no one like him on earth, a man of blameless and upright life, who fears God and sets his face against wrong-doing." (Job 2:3)

Eulogy: Jacob Obadiah Bledsoe

"I have heard the comment attributed to Mark Twain that a man he knew was a "good man in the worst sense of the word." I presume he was speaking of the sort who is generally a pretty good fellow but will never let anybody forget any of the good things he does. Brothers and sisters, there is a thin line between righteousness and self-righteousness and those who cross that invisible border pass from the sunny fields of great virtue to the swamp of deep sin.

Rabbi Akiva said that God allowed the righteous to suffer in this world for their few evil deeds so they might be ready to enter into the joy of the world to come. On the other hand, those who did evil were allowed to bask in the rewards of their few good deeds in this world, since the world to come would be a place of misery for them. *(Genesis Rabbah* 33.1)

"I can tell you from personal experience, however, that J. O. Bledsoe was a good man in the *best* sense of the word. He just went about his business choosing the right way as best he could see it on each and every occasion. He didn't make a big fuss over what he did, and he never seemed to want anybody else to. Now, I'm not going to be so bold as to suggest that his life was without blemish, but I will contend to my last breath that he never desired to do another soul harm. If he had omitted a duty to a neighbor or committed some act that bruised another life, he was quick to make amends. He let his deeds speak of his virtue, for his tongue never would. Although an educated man who could have followed many callings, he was no more puffed up over what he knew than what he did.

"Although he was not of our religion, there was not a soul from any church who would fault him as a husband, father, neighbor, or friend. Years ago he was known to frequent any number of our congregations, though he chose to join none. Sometimes he would attend two services a Sunday. Did you know that? I thought not. I once asked him why he went to church so often, with it not being even his religion, and he told me that he was concerned that his children might stumble from the high road of life, and he was just hoping to make up for any missteps they might make.

Certain of the rabbis portray Job as a member of Pharaoh's inner court at the time the Hebrew slaves were attempting to escape Egypt. At this same time, the wicked angel, Samael, made a case against Israel before God's court and demanded to know why such time and effort were wasted on weak, pitiful creatures like the slaves. Whereupon God turned Job over to Samael, and while this adversary of Israel, God, and Job was busy tormenting a righteous Gentile, the children of Israel escaped through the sea. When they were safe on the other shore, God rescued Job. *(Exodus Rabbah* 21.8)

"As you all know, J. O. was a farmer and a prosperous one, but some can remember, as I surely do, that it was not always so. As the century turned so did the hand of providence turn against J. O. Bledsoe. In 1901 the hog cholera killed every last boar, sow, and shoat on his place. Seems like no

75

sooner were those carcasses disposed of than his entire herd of prize-winning Angus succumbed to some ailment that was never determined. Even the shade trees around his house were stricken by some fungus, lost every last leaf just as his neighbors' were sprouting and stood like huge, spindly skeletons the rest of their days.

"Then the worst calamity that could befall any of God's creatures came his way. In one afternoon, every single one of his children was taken by a twister, the only one to appear that tornado season. They had all gathered for a party, one of their birthdays, I believe. And in "the twinkling of an eye," as the Scripture says, they were no longer. When other men would have ended it all, J. O. held on. There were those in his own family who told him to curse God and die, but J. O. held on. Even after he developed an affliction that literally covered his body with sores—and I am sure he wished he could die—he held on. When there was no earthly reason to hold on, he held on. When it seemed like the devil could do no worse than J. O. had suffered, some friends from our churches came to console him. But he would have nothing of their consolation.

In the bargain with Satan God outwitted that trickster with the command that Job's life must be spared whatever else happened. This put a terrible pressure on the Adversary, since the command was like saying, "You may break the wine bottle, but you must not let the wine spill." (*Sefer Ha-Aggadah* 719. 332)

"J. O. Bledsoe left a diary from that time, and I would like to read selections from that work. It will offer those who knew him and many who did not some knowledge of the workings of his mind and spirit during this time of great distress." *(Michael Williams)*

A Matter of Death and Life

Rather than console him, Job's so-called comforters engage him in a debate about his suffering, and Job responds with a rather dour summary of the human condition.

The Story

Every being born of woman is short-lived and full of trouble. He blossoms like a flower and withers away; fleeting as a shadow, he does not endure; he is like a wineskin that perishes or a garment that moths have eaten. It is on such a creature you fix your eyes, and bring him into court before you! Truly the days of such a one's life are determined, and the number of his months is known to you; you have laid down a limit, which cannot be exceeded. Look away from him therefore and leave him to count off the hours like a hired labourer. If a tree is cut down, there is hope that it will sprout again and fresh shoots will not fail. Though its root becomes old in the earth, its stump dying in the ground, yet when it scents water it may break into bud and make new growth like a young plant. But when a human being dies all his power vanishes; he expires, and where is he then? As the waters of a lake dwindle, or as a river shrinks and runs dry, so mortal man lies down, never to rise until the very sky splits open. If a man dies, can he live again? He can never be roused from this sleep. If only you would hide me in Sheol, conceal me until your anger is past, and only then fix a time to recall me to mind! I would not lose hope, however long my service, waiting for my relief to come.

Comments on the Story

The poem in Job 14 has great literary merit and is sometimes read as an independent composition. But it is best understood in its context as the culmination of the first cycle of speeches (chaps. 3–14) in the dialogue (chaps. 3–27). The narrative relates that when Job's three friends hear of the disasters that have befallen him, each of them leaves his home and travels to Job's land in order to console him. They remain with him for seven days and seven nights and never say a word, showing respect for the enormity of his loss.

But Job forced a dialogue by erupting with a curse on the day of his birth (chap. 3). Job begins the debate in full awareness of his integrity—never once does he imagine that he has done something amiss. Instead of guilt he expresses outrage that life could include such misery. Why is a person born at all if suffering is his or her destiny? Why not prefer death and peace to life and torment? The friends will now respond to this challenge to orthodox piety.

They do so in order: First Eliphaz, the senior statesman, Job's erstwhile peer. He speaks at greater length than do his colleagues, and he begins more gently. But over the course of the three cycles, as his authority is ignored, Eliphaz turns on his friend viciously. The next respondent, Bildad, is a younger man who aspires to the greatness of his elders in the wisdom tradition. Because Job is a defector from this orthodox camp, Bildad can mock him openly and lecture to him condescendingly without penalty. The third friend is Zophar, who claims mystical knowledge of God's ways. Secure in his special revelation, Zophar treats Job's misfortune as if it were a simple matter that could be resolved immediately by doing what Zophar advises.

While the three friends bite at his heels, Job mounts his own strategy for obtaining redress from God: a lawsuit. The entire book shows the influence of Israel's legal system and its methods of obtaining justice between two disputing parties. The essence of this system is justice at the gate, an informal method of trying civil cases. In this process, which is carried out at the city gates (significantly, since this is the threshold of the community), two litigants take turns presenting their version of the problem before the elders of the city, one of whom acts as a judge in the case. The judge decides how the dispute should be settled, and the elders witness the decision and so bring an end to the matter. In cases of extreme difficulty, the elders might bring in an arbitor or seek an oracle from Yahweh through a priest. (An example of justice at the gate can be found in Ruth 4.)

In Job's second speech (chaps. 9–10), he raises the possibility of bringing suit against God for the suffering God has unjustly imposed on him (9:2). Job is familiar with the system, having taken the defense of those without legal status in his own community (29:7-16). But there are difficulties with this proposal: God is both his adversary and his judge; in God's absolute power he is unaccountable to mortals; and God has terrorized Job so much that Job cannot even stand before him. Nevertheless, Job proceeds with his desperate plan, realizing that it is his only hope: "If he wishes to slay me, I have nothing to lose;/ I shall still defend my conduct to his face" (13:15). This is the background in which 14:1-14 must be understood.

There are really two poems in this reading. The first consists of general reflections on the nature of humankind, supported by analogies drawn from nature. Mortal beings, as opposed to the beings who attend God in the heavenly assembly, are mortal and given to trials and tribulation. From the perspective of eternity, the human lifespan is as brief as the bloom of a flower. The translators of the REB have moved a verse from the previous chapter (13:28) to 14:2 to reinforce this point with some vivid imagery. This pitiful human creature is the subject of God's constant surveillance (see 7:8, 17-20; 10:6, 14; 13:27). Job wishes God would just leave him alone so he could spend his few remaining days without terror (see 10:20-22). But he does not, therefore, drop the idea of prosecution. He proceeds from here indirectly.

The second poem starts, as Job often does, with the hopelessness of his situation. Even a tree stump fares better than a human being who has been cut down, for trees can revive themselves, but human beings die and do not rise up again. Job's statements show that the concept of immortality, to which the Egyptians subscribed, was not accepted in Israel, although the realm of the dead (Sheol) implies some sort of continued individual existence. But Job has an audacious plan: If God will just shelter Job in this shadowy nether world until his anger is past, Job will endure until he is called again by God.

Then God's love for his creature (see 10:8-17) would prevail. And then Job could put his case to God and expect to receive real justice. Job, therefore, calls on God's justice to defend him against God's injustice, and God's love for him to defend him against God's destruction of him. Will God act against God's sovereign interests in order to rescue Job? This, rather than immortality, is Job's great hope.

Retelling the Story

"If a man dies, can he live again?
He can never be roused from this sleep.
If only you would hide me in Sheol,
conceal me until your anger is past,
and only then fix a time to recall me to mind!" (Job 14:12b-13)

April 21, 1901

The cholera has taken every single one of my hogs in less than a week. The strange irony of these events is compounded by the fact that I have heard of no other hog farmer who has had even one shoat to pass on from this particular ailment. If others are not dying, how did mine catch it? Will they pass it along to others? I do not know. At least the buds that have burst forth from the trees are beginning to be accompanied by leaves.

Some of the sages suggest that Job was not a historical figure but a character in a parable. They liken the book to the story told by Nathan to David to convict the king of his abuses of power. Others contend, however, that the specific mention of his name and his homeland lend historical credence to Job's story. Still others claim that he was the most righteous Gentile in history and thus he was rewarded so extravagantly by God. (*Sefer Ha-Aggadah* 445.415 and *Genesis Rabbah* 57.4)

May 2, 1901

My life seems to be withering away like the leaves on my oaks and box elders. The leaves that seemed so promising a few days ago turned yellow, then brown, and fell to the ground. I feel like a dried and broken branch, a trunk rotting from the center out. When I go out walking, I watch the ground around my feet to see if I even cast a shadow anymore. Were it not for the grief that never lets up I wouldn't even know that I was still alive. If I did not know better, I would think that God had some grievance against me.

May 15, 1901

Each day we lose more Angus. I awake each morning to find another four or five dead in the pasture or barn. At this rate I will be out of the cattle business altogether by summer's end. First the hogs, then my trees, and now this. I am beginning to ask why this is happening to me. No other farmer in this end of the county has known a single loss of hog, tree, or heifer but me. If this is luck, then it is surely a run of bad. If it is not, God help me. At least I still have my family.

Some later sages could not think of Job as anything but Jewish. He was called "servant of God" and was aid to the household of Jacob. Some say he was Esau's grandson and married Dinah as his second wife. Clearly all this is pious speculation, but the attempt to link Job with the family of a patriarch speaks of the great esteem in which he was held. (Ginzberg II, 225)

May 23, 1901

I feel like a man who is asleep and can't wake up. I might as well be dead. I was taught in school that the ancients thought each life was a thread spun by one of the fates. If that is so, then mine has been cut short in the cruelest way. My life has ended without ending. I am in hell yet still alive. My neighbors who speak of family trees have seen mine hacked down and the roots dug up and burned. There will be no one to remember my ancestors or me because my children are gone—every last one of them. Can a tornado strike as precisely as lightning, taking only one house and one family, and leave the rest of the countryside untouched? Only a twister sent by the devil could drive such sorrow so deep into the heart of a father. It is not that I wish the happiness of others to be destroyed alongside mine. No, I simply want to know in whose warped sense of justice has everything I am and have been taken from me. If this is God's justice, then I want none of it. May God forget that I ever existed and remember me only when this is completed. May I awaken from this nightmare to find that I have only been dreaming.

June 6, 1901

I have gone to live among the refuse since it seems the only fitting place for me. I have been tossed aside like a dead leaf. I have been dragged to a pit and discarded like the carcasses of my hogs and cattle. The blood in my veins has dried up like a river in drought season. My skin is beginning to erupt with boils. Once God was my refuge, but now I have come to sit in the place where the unwanted things of this world are thrown, cursed by a providence I have done nothing to offend. I would curse you in return, unjust judge, but I will not give you the satisfaction of wiping me from the face of the earth until you have offered a few answers to me. Those who were friendly to me before I became a mask of living death say they will come to my aid and comfort. We shall see.

(Michael Williams)

Job's Defender

Job, in a more hopeful mood, expresses the faith that God's justice in the person of a vindicator will prevail over the injustice he has suffered.

The Story

Would that my words might be written down, that they might be engraved in an inscription, incised with an iron tool and filled with lead, carved in rock as a witness! But I know that my vindicator lives and that he will rise last to speak in court; I shall discern my witness standing at my side and see my defending counsel, even God himself, whom I shall see with my own eyes, I myself and no other.

Comments on the Story

So far in the dialogue Job has refused to let his friends become the interpreters of his suffering. In speech after speech, they argue that Job's misery is punishment for his sins and that he must, therefore, repent. Their understanding rests on the traditional wisdom doctrine of retribution—that God rewards the good with prosperity and punishes the wicked with disaster in their lifetime. But the friends apply this general scheme to everday life with a new intensity. To them, the observable fact that Job is suffering indicates without fail that Job is one of the wicked whom God is justly punishing. For Job, the very opposite is true, and no one will listen, hence his complete desperation.

Now that the friends have become Job's betrayers, who will present his case to God for a hearing? Now that God has become Job's enemy, who will hear his pleas? Job's speech in chapter 19 is very similar to his speech in chapters 16–17: Job employs the psalmic form of supplication known as lament. Like the traditional Israelite songs of misery and hope, these speeches begin with a rebuke of his friends' current counsel, complaining that God is his enemy, that his friends and family have turned against him, and alternating between cries of despair and cries of hope (a striking echo of these themes may be found in Psalm 39). The ambivalence of his thoughts makes it difficult to see whether Job's thought is progressing logically, but his sentiments now begin to shift the focus away from the opening exposition of his problems and toward the later chapters of the book, where they will be resolved.

In Job 14:1-4, Job made the desperate suggestion that God hide him in the land of the dead temporarily until his anger passes, and God and Job would be able to address their dispute face to face. Now Job develops an alternative that he hinted at in chapter 9:32-35: If only there were an arbiter *(mokiah)*, someone who could mediate between God and Job until the danger was past, then he could hope for justice from the Almighty. In Job 16:19 he calls for a witness *(ad)* to corroborate his story. And finally in 19:25 he makes a plea for a redeemer *(go'el)* to step forward from the crowd of accusers to defend him.

Christian tradition has cited this short passage as evidence of the doctrine of immortality and has identified the redeemer figure in verse 25 as Christ (e.g., the aria "I Know That My Redeemer Liveth" from Handel's *Messiah*). This no doubt accounts for the presence of this passage in the lectionaries. The apparent denial of immortality in our previous poetic story, Job 14:1-14, rules out the first consideration (at least for a reading at the level of the Hebrew tradition). The second question, whether Job's *go'el* is symbolic of Christ, is sometimes recast into the question of whether Job had a specific kind of savior in mind. Does Job refer to a prototype of the messianic figure in later apocalyptic literature?

The *go'el* does not appear to be such a prototype, though one can understand how the Christian imagination might make that interpretation. After suspecting that his complaint, unacknowledged by God and his companions, will fade into oblivion, Job begins with the wish that his words be permanently inscribed (whether in a book, on a lead tablet, or in rock, the text is unclear). In chapter 16, Job makes a similar request that his blood lie on the ground, thick and unabsorbed, a permanent sign of the injustice committed against him (cf. Gen. 4:10, "Your brother's blood is crying out to me from the ground"). The redeemer or *go'el* is witness of another kind. In Israelite tradition, the *go'el* is the next-of-kin who protects, defends, and pursues vengeance for a relative who is not able to do this for himself or herself. There are homely examples of this function in the Hebrew Bible (2 Sam. 14:4-11; Ruth 4:4-6); on a more exalted plane, Yahweh is often called Israel's redeemer from the bondage of Egypt. Job calls on someone to exercise this function for him, someone to stand (as a witness in a trial) just as the *go'el* in Israel was either a relative or someone who volunteered for this service.

This protective figure is unknown to Job, and therefore can hardly be defined as a quasi-divine personage. The best analogy to Job's wish is found in his final testimony to God in chapters 29–30, where he describes the kind of deliverance that he seeks; it is precisely the protection that he himself once offered the widow, the orphan, and the oppressed. Although unrelated to these destitute persons, and perhaps even unknown to them, he stepped forward to defend them (29:12-17). It is the arrival of salvation from an unexpected and unknown source that Job craves.

Verse 26 cannot be translated with any confidence as to its exact meaning; an equally valid rendering would be "Even after my skin is flayed, Without my flesh I shall see God," or "After . . . my skin is peeled off! But from my flesh I would behold Eloah." This verse seems to express Job's desire to see God face to face in his own lifetime, a goal that would be accomplished if the Redeemer were to assist him. The entire passage, therefore, builds on Job's mounting desire to meet with God and to settle their differences in an orderly, legal way. This is the only antidote to the chaos that Job has experienced in his body as it has been ravaged by the divine warrior.

Retelling the Story

"But I know that my vindicator lives
and that he will rise last to speak in court;
I shall discern my witness standing at my side
and see my defending counsel, even God himself." (Job 19:25-26)

Mid-June 1901

Let them chisel these words on my tombstone: "Though not perfect, he did not deserve what he suffered." That is my first wish. My second is a heartfelt desire that God will create a special hell for those who sit in good health and with families intact and money in their pocket while they explain to others why we suffer. Their personal hell would consist of an eternity of listening to their own words spoken back to them unceasingly. That would be torment enough.

When Job's friends came to visit him, they could not even recognize him because he had been so disfigured by his suffering. And the odor was so bad around where he sat that they ordered perfume to be scattered for four hours before they could get a close enough look at their friend to know it was truly he who sat there. (Ginzberg II, 237)

Later the same day:

What do these religious people want? I followed the rules. I even followed the commandments of other peoples' gods. And what good did it do me? I sit here surrounded by the cast-off articles of the world, a man eaten up with sores having lost everything that makes human life bearable. Now come, tell me that God is just and that I suffer only what

I deserve. Not a single one of the good churchgoing people with whom I sat on the same pews week after week will say a word in my defense. No, they are too busy defending their God from the truth. To them my woes and losses are not simply punishment but the very proof that I deserved them in the first place. I am glad that none of these good folk is my doctor for they would hasten my death, since merely being ill is proof to them of God's disfavor toward me. And I am glad that I do not stand before the judicial bench of any of these theologians, for they would hang me for suffering, and every misfortune would be just another piece of evidence of my guilt. God save me from such murderous healers and hanging judges. God save us all from such religion.

> When asked what the most difficult part of his trials had been Job is reputed to have said, "That those who hate me celebrate my misfortune and suffering." (Ginzberg II, 228)

That same night:

I have given more thought on the subject of my guilt or innocence in this matter of all I have lost. Perhaps, if none of God's henchmen will say a good word for me, I am left with only one recourse. I will call upon the divine judge, who knows my heart better that even I can understand, to be my defense counsel. I know that the One who can vindicate me lives, if not on this earth, then in heaven. I will call upon the One to whom I have prayed, whom I have served, to come and serve as my attorney in this case. I have been not only harmed, but slandered as well. My good name has been taken from me along with my animals, my home, and my children. People look at me and say in their hearts, if not with their lips, "What did he do to come to such a state?" I have done nothing to deserve this! Do you hear me? I will shout it from this rubbish heap. I am not guilty as charged! Let the one who inflicted me come and testify to my integrity. It is all I have left—all I have left.

Later:

Whether it is still night or morning I do not know. I have railed to a silent heaven, and now I sit wrapped in my own silence and wear the night as a cloak. This is the only comfort I will receive, I think. To have all other voices silenced but the still small quiet in which God

85

does not answer. I know that the only One in the universe who can vindi-cate me now lives, but if I cannot hear from the One who can defend me, I will hear from no other.

(Michael Williams)

The Hidden God

Job calls for a trial to determine if his suffering is justified.

The Story

Job answered:
Even today my thoughts are embittered,
for God's hand is heavy on me in my trouble.
If only I knew how to reach him,
how to enter his court,
I should state my case before him
and set out my arguments in full;
then I should learn what answer he would give
and understand what he had to say to me.
Would he exert his great power to browbeat me?

No; God himself would never set his face against me.
There in his court the upright are vindicated,
and I should win from my judge an outright acquittal.
If I go to the east, he is not there;
if west, I cannot find him;
when I turn north, I do not descry him;
I face south, but he is not to be seen.
. . . .
It is God who makes me faint-hearted,
the Almighty who fills me with fear,
yet I am not reduced to silence by the darkness
or by the mystery which hides him.

Comments on the Story

Where is God to be found? Depending on its context, this question can be either naive or profound, reflecting the curiosity of a child or the rigor of a theologian. In the Hebrew Bible there are many potential answers to this question, depending on whether the speaker stands in the tradition of the prophet, the priest, or the wise individual.

In the book of Job, this crucial question is framed by a story in which God is a character and who, at least sometimes, has a definite location. In the prose narrative, God is situated in the heavenly realm as a monarch surrounded by a court and its entourage. God's agent, the Adversary, represents him on earth by means of various images—God's hand, for example, or God's face. Human beings know that God is present on earth in some manner to the extent that they experience the effects of his presence; in addition to the friends' belief that God has been mediated through conventional religious traditions, Eliphaz describes a vision of God in the night (4:12-21), and Elihu believes that God communicates through dreams (33:15-16). Job, however, offers the most stunning testimony to God's presence on earth, claiming that his physical ailments and torment are the manifestations of God as a warrior and as a spy against him. Yet, Job also maintains an ideal vision of God as creator, impartial judge, and friend who has withdrawn from Job's experience. This God exists somewhere, but he is known only through Job's remembrance, loyalty, and hope for the future.

In Job 23:1-9, 16-17, Job has decided to set off in search of his departed, greatly yearned-for deity. Now in the third cycle of dialogues (chaps. 22–27), Job has turned away from his friends and thinks only of his own ills and the plight of humankind seen in this light. But there is continuity with Job's previous utterances, particularly 14:1-14 and 19:25-27, for here Job continues a series of wishes or hopes that alternate with his ringing accusations against God and the friends. All are introduced by the idiomatic expression "If only . . ! " (literally, "Who will give that?"), connected to wishes that something specific would happen to bring resolution to Job's suffering. The first hope is that God would bring his torment to an end by murdering Job outright (6:8-9). The second and third are found in chapters 14 and 19, where Job asks to be hidden in Sheol and then that a redeemer would be found to testify for him. The final hope, that he could see God face to face and present his case before him, is the most aggressive wish because it carries Job's lament to its ultimate limit: a showdown with God.

This text is fraught with textual difficulties—almost as many as in 19:23-27, but without the high stakes in interpretation. The translation of verse 2 in the REB is a good approximation of difficult lines; it would be equally valid to translate the words, "Today my complaint is rebellious" as the RSV has it, and it is not clear whether it is God's hand or "my hand" which is heavy. However we construe the details, this verse does convey the prospect that Job's next proposal will be radical. From his earlier statement that he is ready to speak and contend with God (13:3) but that God is elusive (9:11-12), Job has now determined that he will make his case directly to God, if he can only find God.

Job's hope to locate God and make his case is based on two things: (1) his belief that God can be found in pure presence, available to human sight, and (2) his thorough confidence that his own uprightness will protect him from being destroyed by God's awesome power and purity (see also Isa. 6:1-7). A wicked man, he contends, would not look for God and would not survive divine scrutiny. Therefore, in verses 4-7 he anticipates the trial that would occur when God is actually found, which rests on their prior relationship being restored. But the God Job seeks is not to be found on an earthly plane; he literally looks forward, backward, to the left, and to the right (representing the four compass points), but God is not present.

In the verses that follow, but which have been omitted from the story (10-15),

Job returns to the theme that God has him under surveillance (see also 7:17-20; 13:27), despite his careful religious observance. Regardless of Job's inner resolve and courage, he realizes that God is not bound by the canons of human justice. God may never revoke his sentence against Job even if Job is proven to be in the right. Job's risk in calling for a direct encounter is clear to him once more. Where is God to be found? Although Job will not be silenced (23:17), there is no advantage in pursuit, because God is above all free. There is a hint of the "appearance" of God from the whirlwind (38:1) in this story. If Job finally sees God, it will be when God wants it to happen and what God wants Job to see.

Retelling the Story

> "If only I knew how to reach him,
> how to enter his court,
> I should state my case before him
> and set out my arguments in full." (Job 23:3-4)

A Brief for My Defense:

1. Jacob Obadiah Bledsoe, having no training in legal matters, yet having heard no word from my defense counsel and having already been condemned in the court of public opinion, prepare to make my own defense before the only bench that matters. I am not even sure how I should address the court. "Your honor" is applied to human judges and "Your highness" to royal ones, but my Judge is higher still than both of these. Knowing you are honorable, I will state from the start that I, too, am an honorable man. Knowing little of "highness," I will simply say that I have felt very "low" in recent days. Thus I will address you by the trait to which I will entrust my fate: Your Honesty.

These are the things I have suffered:

1. The loss of my entire holdings in boars, sows, and shoats;

2. the loss of my entire holdings of fine Angus cattle, adults and calves;

3. the loss of every tree on my farm, leaving it unshaded from the heat of the sun;

4. the loss of my seven children all in one hour;

5. the loss of my health, being afflicted by a disease of the skin that is most painful to me and unpleasant to view;

The rabbis say that God gave Job a choice of trials: either suffer the losses he, in fact, did or be poor. Job chose suffering, since poverty is a greater burden than other troubles. *(Exodus Rabbah 31.12)*

89

6. the loss of my home and wife, since I can no longer live with other human company but reside on a refuse dump;

7. and the loss of my faith in religion and religious people, even those who claim to represent you (especially those who claim to represent you!).

> No Gentile was more righteous than Job, but his wealth led him astray, according to the rabbis. Although righteous in his behavior, he is demanding and impudent with God. The sages suggest that the rich are just like that. *(Deuteronomy Rabbah 2.4)*

The things I have done that can be considered worthy of punishment:

1. Lied to others to spare their feelings, but never to intentionally cheat or mislead them;

2. looked upon the beauty of women with desire, yet without even once acting on that impulse;

3. looked upon the holdings of my neighbors with desire, yet without ever taking steps to take anything from them;

4. spoke in anger to my wife and children, yet never without regretting it immediately and seeking their forgiveness;

5. helped my neighbors in a less than selfless fashion, hoping that I could call on them in my time of need;

6. refused to heed sufficiently the cry of those who were in the position of hardship that I hold now;

7. and sought to gain your favor for my children by attending the churches that profess to represent you.

Now, Your Honesty, there is no court on earth that can hear this case. If yours is a court where justice is done, place these lists side by side and tell me whether the two balance. Have I misrepresented my case, or is any article untrue? Have I not received severe punishment for minor infractions? Are not my sufferings cruel and unusual, or have I received just recompense at your hand? Offer me your answer, and I will listen to you.

(Michael Williams)

The Divine Challenge

God answers Job by confronting him with the deep mysteries of creation.

The Story

Then the LORD answered Job out of the tempest:
Who is this who darkens counsel
  with words devoid of knowledge?
Brace yourself and stand up like a man;
I shall put questions to you, and you
  must answer.
Where were you when I laid the earth's
  foundations?
Tell me, if you know and understand.
Who fixed its dimensions? Surely you
  know!
Who stretched a measuring line over it?
On what do its supporting pillars rest?
Who set its corner-stone in place,
  while the morning stars sang in chorus
and the sons of God all shouted for joy?
. . . .

Can you command the clouds
  to envelop you in a deluge of rain?
If you bid lightning speed on its way,
  will it say to you, 'I am ready'?
Who put wisdom in depths of darkness
  and veiled understanding in secrecy?
Who is wise enough to marshal the rain-
  clouds
and empty the cisterns of heaven,
when the dusty soil sets in a dense mass,
and the clods of earth stick fast together?
Can you hunt prey for the lioness
  and satisfy the appetite of young lions,
as they crouch in the lair
or lie in wait in the covert?
Who provides the raven with its quarry
  when its fledglings cry aloud,
  croaking for lack of food?

Comments on the Story

Since Job and his friends have debated through the better portion of the book over the correct interpretation of Job's suffering, a pronouncement from some higher authority has a certain appeal; it would draw this debate to a close and solve the matter like a riddle. In fact, the appearance of God, or the theophany (Job 38–41), only opens further questions: Why doesn't God account for his persecution of Job? Why does God seem to bully rather than console the sufferer? Why does God speak as the Creator rather than as the Lord of history? These are natural questions, given the expectations raised in the previous chapters of the book. But as we have seen, the book of Job is not a systematic exposition of the nature of evil, nor is it a straightforward narrative account of the redemption of an innocent sufferer. In terms of structure and meaning, the book of Job follows its own rules.

If we wish to penetrate the meaning of the speeches of God (there are two, 38–39 and 40:6–41:34), the first thing to notice is the fact that they happen at all. God's speech from the whirlwind is a deeply shocking event. Job as a character has had no preparation for it, although his wish to confront God face to face has echoed through the dialogue. The friends would have been outraged that a sinful man would not be punished immediately. A more conventional author might have broken into narrative at this point, combining elements from Israel's famous theophanies, such as Jacob's ladder, Moses and the burning bush, Sinai, or even Elijah's encounter with "a still small voice." The book of Job might have ended with the story of how Job wandered as an exile until he came upon a sacred grove of trees, and there had a vision that revealed the end of his oppression by God and the beginning of a new life. The narrator could have chosen to quote God's words in the vision, so that the reader might hear the redemptive message and take it to heart. Nothing wrong with that. But the poet has a more ambitious plan. The God of the opening narrative who sat on his throne in heaven surrounded by his host now surfaces (descends?) as a character in the dialogue—one of the dialogue partners. With this act, we are reminded about the moral ambiguity of God's character. Now that God has finally chosen to speak, it becomes clear that God has been present all along, hearing and observing Job's anguish but remaining deliberately hidden from human view.

The God of the divine speeches is a character in a parable, but he specifically carries the name of Israel's own deity, Yahweh. Elsewhere in the book God is called Eloah or Shaddai. Both of these names are ancient and venerable titles for Yahweh, but they are to be distinguished clearly from the special name God revealed to Moses. When Yahweh speaks, therefore, it is Israel's God revealing himself to Job, a foreigner, in a work of fiction set in a time long before the time of Moses. The use of the name is a signal to the original readers of Job that their own religious beliefs have a universal significance. By making Yahweh speak, the sages of Israel have devised a way for the wisdom tradition to uphold and console the people of Israel in their grief over the loss of Jerusalem, just as the prophets and the priests did in their own way.

Communities no less than individuals suffer without cause and look to God for answers to bitter, existential questions. This lends gravity to Yahweh's refusal to address Job's charges or to account for his persecution. Instead Yahweh poses questions: Who are you to question my design *('esah)* of the world? Who are you to question my justice *(mispat)*? The first question is addressed by our lection. God responds to Job's superhuman accusations of God by attacking Job's superhuman status. Is Job not a mere mortal, and, therefore, utterly removed from divine activity, such as the creation and maintenance of the world and all its creatures? Job is only a man, and, therefore, was not present when God as a master builder laid out the foundations of the world, to the joyful praise of the cohort in heaven—unlike Wisdom, who was present at the world's creation (see Prov. 8:22-31), Job was not there. Again, Job is not in control of storms, which were usually brief and violent and thus associated in the ancient Near East with divinity. Job does not control the ecosystem of hunters and prey; therefore, he cannot provide for lions or keep the generations of ravens alive from year to year. God's power is manifested in the wisdom that is buried within all living things, driving them on to be uniquely themselves (cf. Job 28).

For all their ambiguity, the divine speeches are Job's definitive answer. But it is not just the words that are important, but the manner in which they approach Job and—even more important—the way in which Job receives them. God's questions are not posed from an armchair in the study; God breaks in on Job with the fury of a whirlwind and a voice of challenge to Job's defiance. The storm from which God speaks is not off in the distance somewhere. Job is actually inside it, receiving images of creation that overwhelm him and hearing that his stubbornness in pursuing his case against God is not appropriate. God's very presence is a furious and fascinating power that mocks Job's attempt to stand on his own, even as the wind whips around his body. God, the mystery that both terrifies and draws Job to itself, has communicated itself to Job as a presence that is deeply embedded in the world and its rhythms. It is thus a matter of seeing things right. In this whirlwind, hearing words of challenge and seeing visions of the strange and marvelous patterns of creation, Job the devastated recognizes the Other whom he has sought. Another man may have seen only the storm.

Retelling the Story

"Who put wisdom in depths of darkness
and veiled understanding in secrecy?" (Job 38:36)

A Time Out of Time

In the heart of the night (what time of day I do not know), I have faced the depths and lived to tell the tale. There was a storm last night, whether within or without or both I cannot tell. All I can tell you is that I heard the heartbeat that keeps our universe in motion and saw with my own eyes the dark body that encompasses our world. This place we call earth is but a cell in this larger body whose workings I can no more know than a flake of my wretched skin can know all the systems that make up J. O. Bledsoe. I can no more discern the mind of my Maker than a splinter from a fence rail could know the design or purpose of the barriers I placed on the perimeter of my now useless farm. What I heard was the

93

deafening roar of my own confusion and ignorance. What I saw was the thick, dank cloud of my own unknowing.

Three times in the biblical record the winds blew beyond the force anyone had ever seen before or since. Once was during the storm that almost swamped the ship that carried Jonah. The second time was the wind in which Elijah did not hear the voice of God. And the third time was the wind from which Job did hear God's voice. (Genesis Rabbah 24.4 and Leviticus Rabbah 15.1)

I have heard the pious ask, "Is there a word from the Lord?" Now I know that they had no idea what they were requesting. Were they asking for their entire being to be disassembled like one of their implements for farming, then to be reassembled into an entirely different contraption? I think not! Yet that is the result of a word from the Lord. I have heard preachers say that they had "a word from the Lord" for their congregations. Had they any knowledge that a word from the Lord would bury them under the earth to die like an acorn, planted only to sprout forth as a tree as different from the acorn as the oak? I think not! All who have spoken so glibly of a word from the Lord have spoken in utter ignorance. I include myself in that number.

I got what I asked for, but not what I wanted. I asked for a trial and, believe me, this night has been a trial. I asked to hear God's case but instead I came face-to-face with my defender-prosecutor-judge all in one. All my arguments dissolved under the acid of God's questions: "Where were you . . . ? Where were you . . . ? Where were you . . . ?"

When God had finished speaking to Job, God gave the one who had suffered so greatly a present. This gift consisted of three bands to tie around his waist. When he put even one of them on, his pain disappeared and he forgot all his suffering and loss. When he divided his property among his sons and daughters, Job gave one of these bands to each of his daughters (Ginzberg II, 240-241)

I was nowhere. In my arrogance, I was a child humming a nursery tune to keep from fearing the dark. I was a swaggering braggart ashamed of facing his own shadow. I was a schoolboy who, getting his first lesson, thinks he knows the entire subject.

I was nowhere . . .
I was nowhere . . .
I was nowhere . . .
I was not there when all this

great cawing, croaking, laughing, snarling, whining, yapping, weeping, growling, crowing, singing, and sighing creation came to be. And I will not be invited to its final performance. I am simply a minor character in a great drama. I have no lines, no answers, no questions. Perhaps a glance at the audience is all I am allowed. Yet in that moment my face will shine and they will ask, "Is it just the light or has he, like Moses, seen more that words can say?" They will not know. But I will know.

When the storm was finished, I was drenched, whether from rain or tears or both I cannot say. As the clouds moved and the moon appeared, I thought I could hear, faintly like the raucous voices of children at play, the raven's young calling for food.

(Michael Williams)

Job's Submission

Job, a changed man, bows down before the mysterious presence of God.

The Story

Job answered the LORD:
I know that you can do all things
    and that no purpose beyond you.
You ask: Who is this obscuring
    counsel yet lacking knowledge?
But I have spoken of things
    which I have not understood,
things too wonderful for me to know.
Listen, and let me speak. You said:
I shall put questions to you, and you
    must answer.
I knew of you then only by report,
    but now I see you with my own eyes.
Therefore I yield,
    repenting in dust and ashes.
. . . .
. . .when he had interceded for his
    friends.

The LORD restored Job's fortunes,
and gave him twice the possessions he
had before. All Job's brothers and sisters and his acquaintance of former
days came and feasted with him in his
home. They consoled and comforted
him for all the misfortunes which the
LORD had inflicted on him, and each of
them gave him a sheep and a gold ring.
Thus the LORD blessed the end of Job's
life more than the beginning: he had
fourteen thousand sheep and six thousand camels, a thousand yoke of oxen,
and as many she-donkeys. He also had
seven sons and three daughters; he
named his eldest daughter Jemimah,
the second Keziah, and the third Keren-
happuch. There were no women in all
the world so beautiful as Job's daughters; and their father gave them an
inheritance with their brothers.

Thereafter Job lived another hundred
and forty years; he saw his sons and
his grandsons to four generations, and
he died at a very great age.

Comments on the Story

The conclusion of Job forms a ring around the entire book, but at no point
does it offer simple lessons for the storyteller. In the opening scene in heaven,
God called the Adversary's attention to Job and his exemplary virtue and piety.
The Adversary suggested that Job's service to God was not completely selfless;
they agreed to test this proposal by carrying out dreadful attacks on Job's life
and person. The indifference to morality demonstrated by this project is apparent to the reader but not to the characters of the drama, who must interpret the
raw data of Job's losses in an attempt to discern the inner spirit of the deity.

When God is finished making his speeches, Job knows no more about his predicament than he did before. Nor as compensation does God explain the secrets of the universe. The shock of recognition at first silences Job (40:3-5), and then leaves him with a choice to make; given that God's lack of interest in justice for Job has become patently clear, will Job praise or renounce him? Job finally has the chance, in the Adversary's words, to "curse God to his face." Job does not curse, but what he does offer is less than a hearty blessing. Job's answer, like God's appearance, is ambiguous.

Some readers of this conclusion would say that Job submits to God completely; others that he is reconciled to God once more.

Still others regard their encounter as an indication that Job's inner disposition was still defiant, although his words were respectful. Rather than make a decision on one of these options, the storyteller may wish to preserve the reticence of the biblical writer, who, like other great Israelite narrators, describes the words and actions of characters and permits the reader to supply the precise shading of their thoughts, feelings, or moods.

The second response of Job (42:1-6) is resolutely formal in nature. Job declares what he has concluded from God's speeches: that God's power is unlimited and his purposes will be accomplished—statements characteristic of praise. He quotes God's initial challenge to him, "Who is this obscuring counsel yet lacking knowledge?" (38:2) and responds that God's works are too marvelous for him to speak of. Again, in formal legal fashion, he repeats the second challenge to him, "I shall put questions to you, and you must answer" (38:3). And responds: Before I had only heard of you, but now I see you. Therefore—and the entire book stands poised at this moment—Job says that he yields and repents ("in dust and ashes"). This may signify the ash heap in which Job is sitting, or it may be a reference to Job's awareness of his humanity. An alternate reading of the text would be that Job repents "from dust and ashes," meaning that Job has decided to quit his posture of mourning to rejoin the rest of society. Again, the storyteller may choose between any of these options.

To be sure, this is just a report of the exchange between Job and God, not an interpretation of it. But the storyteller must take care to search for the overall sense of Job's encounter with God rather than depend on details of translation or infer Job's mental state too quickly. After Job witnesses the presence of the deity, he quiets his aggression toward God. In legal terms, he withdraws his lawsuit; in theological terms, he repents—that is, he turns back from his contrary direction and submits to God's higher plan, of which he still knows nothing; in literary terms, he has a profound change of heart.

The Adversary, therefore, has lost the wager once and for all. Job has indeed feared God for nothing, because Job both acknowledged God's sovereignty and experienced firsthand that he could not profit from it. As long as Job, like

97

the friends, was wedded to a scheme of cosmic justice that humans could understand and, therefore, hold God accountable for, God was not truly free. God's freedom was contaminated by the human investment in divine justice, which was especially evident as they called it down on one another in judgment. By appearing but not responding directly to Job's cries for a hearing on charges, God calls Job to a genuine act of faith. Job responds with words of pure self-emptying. The idea that his words might mask a contrary set of feelings removes his integrity from the act, and does not seem to be the case. But again, it is important to note that those who impute sarcasm to Job can never really be proven wrong. The story of Job's testing by heaven is now over; God has won. And as the friends have learned that suffering does not point to sin, Job has learned that his suffering does not mean that God is his enemy. The following narrative is best considered epilogue, and once again we are given words and deeds but no inner motivation. God appears to the friends and commands them to carry out a ritual of reconciliation, if they can persuade Job to offer sacrifice for them. The love and dignity in Job's acceptance of their plea is never stated in the story, but it is unmistakable. The powerful intercession of the victim for his persecutors is an indication of Job's newfound spiritual vigor, and the restoration of his riches simply completes that circle.

Once again, external things stand for inner, spiritual reality. Job's daughters are beautiful and strong (receiving an inheritance of their own puts them on a different footing than most women in Israelite society), an outward and visible sign of Job's inner grace. We are left to infer just how Job, the friends, his brothers and sisters, and his new family might understand Job's ordeal and his journey back from it. This is fertile ground for the storyteller. In the end, Job dies a good death, surrounded by his grandchildren and their grandchildren. The end of Job's life appears to be as conventional as its beginning, but those who accompany Job on his journey to God's presence know that he has been utterly changed. The book's challenge to all storytellers is to express the essence of that change.

Retelling the Story

And their father gave them [his daughters] an inheritance with their brothers. (Job 42:15*b*)

Eulogy: Jacob Obadiah Bledsoe *(continued)*

"So, dear friends, there is his story told in his words. It has been so many years from that disastrous time that many who knew J. O. saw only his recent prosperity. Many whose memory might not go that far back viewed him only as an honest, decent man who never darkened a church door. Many other ministers were bewildered by his virtue mixed with his disdain for all churches and representatives of organized religion. Some even chose to criticize privately, if not publicly, his lack of support for the churches he had frequented before his season of suffering. They thought his faith had been destroyed with his fortune but had not been restored with it. I am here to tell you they were wrong.

When Job was made whole again and his fortunes restored, the rabbis say that he went back to the line of work he followed before his trials; he collected money for the poor. (Ginzberg II, 240)

"It is true that J. O. Bledsoe was a changed man after his trials. Who would not be? But it was more than the hurts and losses of his life that caused his transformation. I have seen people suffer and become stronger by their tribulations, and I have seen others sink into an abyss of bitterness from the same kinds of sorrow or even much less. The soul we remember today was not a bitter man, and although he was stronger for what he had suffered, the change that came over his life was so complete that strength hardly begins to tell of it. I dare to call that change conversion, but of a different sort than any I had ever seen.

"For the new J. O. Bledsoe, there would again be trees blooming in the spring and the sound of cattle on distant hills, and the unmistakable odor of hogs resting through the heat of the day in wallows. There would even be the screams and shouts of children. Although not nearly of the years of Abraham and Sarah, J. O. and his wife saw the birth of seven more children. But when he would speak of them, or sometimes even in his gazing upon them, there seemed to come into his face a mixture of grief and fear. His new family could not help reminding him of those lost, who would never be replaced. And he would never dislodge the deep terror that even these could be ripped from his bosom in an instant.

"For the new J. O. Bledsoe there would never again be simple answers to the questions of life. When he would hear idle explanations on the street or at the feed store about some occasion of grief in the life of a neighbor, he would reply, "Maybe; maybe not." The same was his retort when preachers like me would attempt to talk to him about God's plan of grace for the righteous and God's punishment reserved for the wicked. There are those who will tell you that he was an atheist. There are those who will tell you that he lost all faith in God. Untrue! Untrue! If he had lost faith, it was in people who wanted to stand in the place of God and judge their neighbors by the sorrow in their lives.

"I will end where I began: J. O. Bledsoe was a good man in the only sense of the word that has any meaning, a good man who never expected to be rewarded by others or God for his goodness. A changed man who included his daughters in his will along with his sons; a changed man who cherished all that he

Some sages say that Job's tenacity in calling out to God meant a great defeat for Satan and was the reason for Satan's exclusion from God's presence. When Job finally died, he was mourned by the whole land, but especially by the poor, widows, and orphans. (Ginzberg II, 242)

loved because he knew how easily they could all be lost. I'm here to tell you that he prayed until the end of his days, and I know. You see, he prayed for me. I was one of those preachers who came to him in his grief and placed the blame on his shoulders. Whether I was trying to protect God or myself I cannot say. But I will say today that I was wrong. I was one of those good men in the worst sense of the word. When I told J. O. that I would pray for him it was an accusation, not a word of love.

"Now I know better. Now I can say, 'Brother J. O., pray for me wherever you are today; pray for us all.' " *(Michael Williams)*

III. Ecclesiastes:

A Narrative Introduction

With Ecclesiastes we have reached a new stage of reflection on the truths of human experience to which the sages dedicated themselves. The added dimension is the fact that by the time this book was written, the sages' tradition was itself old and venerable and was, therefore, a subject of reflection and critique. The Speaker in Ecclesiastes pits his experience and ideas against orthodox wisdom in order to reach his own conclusions about the meaning of life. He speaks on his own experiences and uses them to mount a devastating critique of the main ideas in the old wisdom tradition (as found primarily in the book of Proverbs). The Speaker's main conclusion is that human existence is fleeting and insubstantial—there is no lasting profit in any human endeavor. The usual assumptions about the meaning of life must be abandoned; his sharp powers of observation and his dedication to ultimate truth push him to the limit, beyond which there is only suicide or renewal. The Speaker chooses the second option, but couches it in terms of radical simplicity. In the end, there is only the endurance of bad times and the acceptance of good times, which are both a gift of God. This is life in the "now" without certainty about life's mysteries but having the conviction that nothing in life is inalienably one's own. The final wisdom, for the Speaker, allows him to look like a fool to those who are busy accumulating possessions, good works, and even religious truth. The hunger to know, to be wise, is just another appetite to satisfy.

Ecclesiastes is one of the most mysterious books in the Hebrew Bible. It was originally untitled, as were most of the books of the Bible, but acquired a name based on an editorial addition to the beginning of the book, which identifies the identity of the book's author, in Hebrew, as Qoheleth (1:1). This Qoheleth is identified as the son of David, king in Jerusalem, and from this was assumed to be Solomon, in honor of that king's role as patron of Israelite wisdom. The name Solomon never actually appears in the book itself. Solomon could not have been the author of Ecclesiastes, however, because the Hebrew in which the book was composed shows signs of being more recent than the tenth century in which Solomon lived. In fact, the book belongs to an era seven hundred years later, in the late Persian/early Greek period of Israelite history (mid-third century, i.e., 250 B.C.E.). Ironically, however, it is probably the association with Solomon that won the book a solid place in the Jewish canon.

"Ecclesiastes" is the Greek translation of a Hebrew word, *qoheleth*. The form of the word, a feminine participle, denotes occupation or function. The idea of Qoheleth as an activity rather than a name is reinforced by the addition of a definite article to the participle in 7:27 and 12:8, making it the Qoheleth. The Qoheleth, or the Speaker (or more traditionally, the Preacher), is a teacher or sage who calls into assembly. The Hebrew root, *qhl,* means to gather or assemble either people or, in this case, perhaps even different forms of wisdom for reflection. Beyond this, the author of the book is unknown; even the word *qoheleth* does not appear elsewhere in the Hebrew Bible.

The literary form of the book has also been a mystery to its readers. Parts of the book bear a strong resemblance to the Egyptian genre of "royal testament," in which didactic poems of varying lengths are put into the mouth of a fictional royal personage as a device to set forth the accumulated wisdom of a sage. Ecclesiastes is a series of short poems that revolve around a few central themes rather than a narrative or a logically constructed lecture. It also contains several other wisdom genres—for example, the saying or proverb ("Futility, utter futility . . . everything is futile"; "The laughter of fools is like the crackling of thorns under a pot"); the "better than" saying ("Better the end of anything than the beginning; better patience than pride!"); the observation ("One more thing I have observed here under the sun: swiftness does not win the race nor strength the battle"); plus others, including the metaphor, the parable, biographical narrative, the beatitude, the woe-cry, and allegory. The Speaker's use of all these wisdom forms puts him squarely into the wisdom tradition, even if he uses these forms to mount an attack on conventional wisdom ideas.

Ecclesiastes has both fascinated and repelled religious thinkers throughout the centuries. The author's vision of the world is darkly pessimistic: There is no discerning the meaning of life through the power of reason; humankind cannot control the future or escape death; God is remote, inaccessible, and essentially dispassionate concerning human existence and its travails. Still, a strange freedom is connected to the acceptance of these truths: Even if human beings and God inhabit separate spheres altogether, God is still in control of the world, and although he doles out pain and suffering, he also offers moments of simple pleasure and peacefulness connected to family life and work. These are to be accepted wholeheartedly as the "portion" allotted by God to God's creatures. So even if the Speaker's message serves to detach humankind from the traditional hope that God protects the human investment in its own well-being, it is not completely nihilistic.

The key to the Speaker's procedure in establishing this message is the meaning of the phrase associated with the book: "Futility, utter futility . . . everything is futile!" The Hebrew word *hebel* has been traditionally translated "vanity," but the current English sense of that word no longer corresponds to the sense of the Hebrew word. *Hebel* is a noun meaning "vapor" or "breath." It signifies anything that is ephemeral or insubstantial, something done to no purpose. The REB's "futility" is a good way to express it; a more literal translation that preserves the original power of the metaphor is R. B. Y. Scott's rendering in the Anchor Bible: "Breath of a breath! The slightest breath! All is a breath!" The repetition is meant to imply the supreme superlative, as the Song of Songs means "the best of songs." It is a pronouncement of utter negation that fills the soul with the sounds of loss and sadness. Yes, it seems to say, another disappointment.

But there is more to console the reader of this work than the rather austere message of the "portion" of simple pleasures, or even the unexpected inheritance that may come to the wise man or the fool. And that is the example of the Speaker himself, who set for himself the lonely quest for meaning. Even though, after all his searching, the Speaker found only a bare thread of happiness in life, he shows great courage in undertaking the task of honestly assessing human existence. We may assume that few could bear the loss of illusion this entailed in his own time, just as few will take to heart the Speaker's message today.

This quest reveals its own deeper blessing. The loss of meaning, like a devastating illness, when it is received with a probing and questioning spirit, can reveal the greatest beauty in life. And one who accepts the task of seeing clearly through deceptions of all kinds can—if he or she chooses—raise a prophetic voice in his or her community. Ecclesiastes represents a sophisticated level of theological thinking in Judaism. The Speaker's yearning for the truth, regardless of where that leads and what it does to orthodox religious views, makes him a maverick and, in essence, a mystic. The road he takes to insight corresponds to the *via negativa* in other great religious traditions. The fewer claims he makes on God and God's part in human existence, the more he exposes the immediate experience of human life. Granted, when he sifts through this immediate experience for something—anything—of lasting benefit, he finds nothing. Yet, it is clear that the Speaker prizes life and the search for meaning. In the end, the usual distractions of the world—wealth, power, status, possessions—have no claim on his soul. Ecclesiastes is the handbook for anyone who would learn spiritual detachment.

So the Speaker, like Job, seeks to rid himself of lesser truths in order to reach the one truth that can reorient his life. Wisdom, with its many-faceted vision of the good life, faces trial for its shortcomings, which merely aid human self-deception. It stands accused of two things: First, wisdom has assumed a specious predictability about the future, and second, it preaches the "two ways" of wisdom and folly but obscures the ultimate dichotomy between life of any kind and the obliteration of death. By denying the positive value of traditionally worthwhile things, calling them "futile" and "without profit," the Speaker pares away illusion. When the deception is gone, no matter how painfully it has passed, the reader/disciple is left to look for the simple pleasure that is given by God and gauge how well this gift is received. The reader who follows the Speaker on his tour of meaninglessness can discover the well-springs of his or her own hope and the foundations on which it is built.

The Futility of Life

Qoheleth, the Speaker, is overwhelmed by the emptiness of human achievements.

The Story

Futility, utter futility, says the Speaker, everything is futile. . . . I, the Speaker, ruled as king over Israel in Jerusalem; and I applied my mind to study and explore by means of wisdom all that is done under heaven. It is a worthless task that God has given to mortals to keep them occupied. I have seen everything that has been done here under the sun; it is all futility and a chasing of the wind. . . . I came to hate all my labour and toil here under the sun, since I should have to leave its fruits to my successor. What will the king's successor do? Will he do what has been done before? Who knows whether he will be wise or foolish? Yet he will have in his control all the fruits of my labour and skill here under the sun. This too is futility. Then I turned and gave myself up to despair, as I reflected on all my labour and toil here under the sun. For though someone toils with wisdom, knowledge, and skill he must leave it all to one who has spent no labour on it. This too is futility and a great wrong. What reward does anyone have for all his labour, his planning, and his toil here under the sun? His lifelong activity is pain and vexation to him; even in the night he has no peace of mind. This too is futility.

Comments on the Story

Our introduction to the Speaker and his message begins in the middle of things with the book's motto or basic theme: "Futility, utter futility . . . everything is futile!" The verse before (1:1) gives the title of the book, for all intents and purposes; this "Speaker" (Hebrew, *Qoheleth*) is claimed to be David's son, king in Jerusalem. While this verse is probably the addition of an editor who wants to give the following, sometimes shocking, book stature and authority to its prospective readers, it helps us to become oriented to the literary device of the "royal testament," which will form the bulk of this reading. Is the Speaker really a king, as he claims to be (note that even the editor does not actually name him Solomon)? We can say confidently that the writer was not Solomon himself, and we know that there were no bonafide kings in Jerusalem when scholars think, based on linguistic evidence for the Hebrew, that the book was written (mid-third century B.C.E.). But as to the royal nature of the Speaker's observations, when the Speaker assumes the persona of a king the reader can perhaps more readily accept the importance of "experience" as the basis for criticism of received truths. This is not just any old experience; it is the experience of a king. It helps the Speaker to be king in the same way that it helps Job to be exceedingly wealthy and pious; in the eyes of the world, their word is good.

The Speaker's first statement in the book is a stern summary: Everything is pointless. It is a foregone conclusion, something the Speaker already knows, and he will tell us how he arrived at the conclusion. This Speaker is, possibly, standing in the street in the marketplace with a small group of interested listeners nearby. An old man is dressed as a sage. He acquires their attention in the time-honored way with the sages in Israel, with the all but unconscious movements that beckon them with the promise of an insight, a reminder of their responsibilities, a clever riddle, or a parable to bring home and tell their wives. But this commanding figure draws himself up to his full height, lets the space around the group grow silent, and begins with only one word, repeated again and again. As he says the word *hevel,* they are suddenly aware of the rising and falling of their own chests. It is involuntary, regular, and shallow. A single breath—inhale, exhale—is almost nothing. Can he really mean that "the everything" *(hacol),* the cosmos itself, is nothing more than this faint wind, this vapor?

We also need verse 3 if we are to get the full impact of the Speaker's opening words. What profit is there, he continues, for anyone in all the effort and struggle of this life? The listeners' ears are caught by this word, "profit," because it means something specific to them. It is what is left for them in their business after all the expenses have been paid; it is their reward after the long day's work. To take this from them—now this is serious. What the Speaker appears to mean here is that their "labour and toil here under the sun" is a metaphor for their whole lives. The expression "under the sun" in particular has a literary sweep to it; some of the Speaker's listeners might be familiar with the Gilgamesh Epic and its memorable line, "Only the gods [live] forever under the sun. As for mankind, numbered are their days; whatever they achieve is but the wind." Yes, the Speaker means to talk about the universe. Generations come and go; the sun rises and sets; the wind blows; water flows. All of this is as involuntary as breath and just as tedious. Look, there is absolutely nothing new in any of it.

Now the actual lection resumes, picking up the Speaker's discourse just as he describes himself as king over Israel in Jerusalem. This claim of grandeur by the old man might even provoke gentle laughter, but by now the listeners know the Speaker is leading them to some new insight. The king is by tradition the patron and protector of wisdom, following the example of Solomon, who was, as history told them, world-renowned for his sagacity. So they are willing to let him be king and find out what the king knows.

The "King of Israel" describes an experiment that he conducted to see if he could find any "profit" or lasting satisfaction in specific human activities (1:12-18). But it is not a proper experiment, because the results have already been determined. Instead, it provides him with an opportunity to catalogue all the usual candidates for human obsession and to find each of them wanting. Our reading omits this litany of disappointments, which includes wisdom and folly, pleasure and enjoyment, and great works. They are all, in his experience, futile and a chasing (or shepherding) of the wind.

The Speaker concludes forcefully, but the effect is far short of Job's empassioned curse on the day of his birth. The Speaker says that he hates life (v. 17), since all effort is simply pointless effort and nothing but trouble. And, as our passage resumes, he repeats his statement: He hates all his labor and toil—and why? Because the reward for his hard work ultimately goes, for when he dies he must leave it to his successor. Now the listeners may suspect that there is some combination of circumstances that might please the Speaker and renew his faith in the system of dying and leaving an inheritance to your offspring. But no, all the variations on this theme are negative: Poverty, of course, is bad; but wealth, if you don't enjoy it, is also bad. It's bad if you don't have an heir to leave your fortune to, and bad if you don't inherit. Here, the evil is an inability to control one's wealth after death and the reality that inherited wealth may do little to strengthen the character of one's successor. The Speaker seems to know that there are no provisions the king can make that will protect his legacy from the depredations of human greed. Like it or not, the heir will have control over the money, if not over himself or herself.

The next two verses show us an interesting train of thought by the Speaker, for he is working from the universal assumption of meaninglessness to the practical, everyday experience of restlessness and the ennui that everyone has sometimes, even if they would describe themselves as happy in general. As he gives up control of the fruit of his labor, the Speaker gives himself up to despair. Having wealth does not protect one, and even having wisdom along with wealth cannot avert one's fate of dying and surrendering control. The listeners must agree. Is it not an egregious wrong to work hard and yet have final control over nothing? Imagine our long hours, our endless search for ways to maximize our profit not only for ourselves but for our dependents as well—eventually they will have it all, and they will not even have to pause to consider where it came from and at what great sacrifice it was won! That thought, once it worms its way fully into the minds of the listeners, can spoil the generous sentiments of even the most devoted business owner. And so the Speaker moves in for the final blow: Your work, how satisfying is it as an ultimate value in life? For at its core lies this lack of control, which steals meaning from even the longest-term perspective. And so your everyday living is infected with nothing but pain and vexation. You should realize, the Speaker seems to say, exactly where this comes from.

The Speaker claims to have given himself up to despair. And here we find the challenge for the storyteller. What manner of story conveys what is actually taking place in the Speaker's mind? Or, in our dismay with this difficult message, should we use a story to attempt to "make straight what is crooked" in Ecclesiastes? Theologians have wrestled with analogous questions; commentators on Ecclesiastes have found at times that the book's skepticism either validates their own questions about life's meaning or that it fills them with admiration for the Speaker's courage and yet gratitude for their own sense of religious security, which removes them from his dilemma. Whatever sense we get from this book, it is better to resist the strong urge to fault Ecclesiastes for not having answers that we believe we have—at least for the present. If we wish to understand the Speaker's concept of the "portion" allotted by God to humankind, and its potential for showing genuine goodness in human life, then we must accept the Speaker's challenge to see the futility at the core of our daily activities and ideas, and strive toward the greater truths that he wants to teach us. Ecclesiastes, as with all literature, poses questions that stories can best answer. But, in turn, stories provoke more questions.

Retelling the Story

Ecclesiastes is the "scroll" *(megillah)* that Jews read on the holiday of Sukkot. This is a joyous fall festival commemorating the wandering of the Jews through the desert, living in booths *(sukkahs)*, after the Exodus, and also celebrating the time of the harvest. Sukkot is one of three pilgrimage holidays when Jews journeyed to Jerusalem. Just as soon as Yom Kippur, the most solemn and holiest of days, ends, and after one breaks the fast, it is time to begin building the *sukkah* for the holiday which begins four days later. This is part of the rhythm of Jewish life. One holiday of life review and repentence flows into the adjoining holiday of joy and celebration. The yearly cycle forms a continuum without an interruption.

Many rabbis identified Qoheleth (translated "the Speaker" here) as Solomon. They say the Hebrew word usually translated "singers," to indicate some of Qoheleth's servants, should really be translated "demons." Also, one of those demons deposed Solomon for a time. As Solomon traveled through the world, most people thought he was mad and refused to believe he was king or any other figure of any importance. It was during this exile from the court, these rabbis suggest, that Solomon penned the work that came to be called Qoheleth. *(Sefer Ha-Aggadah* 130.122)

"Futility, utter futility, says the Speaker, everything is futile. . . . His lifelong activity is pain and vexation to him; even in the night he has no peace of mind. This too is futility" (Eccles. 1:2; 2:23).

So what do we do with our experiences, if everything is foreordained and the only certainty is death? To what end life? Perhaps what we must do is enjoy and appreciate what we have when we have it and use our material goods and the good sense in right ways.

There was once an honest merchant who prospered in all that he did. But he was never satisfied and always complained that things were not good enough. As time went on, his business success began to change. Slowly, slowly he began to earn far less profit. In fact, he made barely enough to pay his bills.

One day, as he was walking through the street, Elijah the Prophet approached him and greeted him. *"Sholom aleikhem,* my friend. Tell me, how are you? I see from the way you are walking that you are filled with worry."

"Aleikhem sholom," answered the merchant. "You are correct. I cannot hide my worry, for my business is not going as well as it should."

Elijah answered, "My friend, you should not worry so much. Things could be far worse. After all, you still earn a living." And Elijah disappeared.

Some time passed and the merchant lost all his livelihood, all his business. He had to borrow money from others. What else could he do?

One day Elijah met the merchant and asked, "My friend, how are things going with you?"

The merchant answered, "Terrible! Worse than ever, for I am so ashamed that I have to live on money from others."

Elijah replied, "Don't worry, for things could be far worse." And again Elijah disappeared.

More time passed. The merchant had borrowed money from everyone he knew and still his debt grew. Soon no one wanted to lend him money or even to meet him on the street.

Once more Elijah met the merchant and asked how he was faring. The merchant answered, "I will tell you the truth: I would now be willing to eat at other people's homes and to live on borrowed money, but now there is not a single person who wants to lend me anything more."

Elijah replied, "Don't complain, because things could be far worse."

And the merchant said, "How could things be worse?"

But when he looked up, he realized that he was talking to himself, as Elijah had vanished.

Now the merchant began to go out begging for charity, since none of his former friends or business merchants wanted anything to do with him. He felt ashamed to go knocking on doors and begging.

And when he met Elijah, he told him the state of his affairs. And Elijah again assured him, "My friend, things could be far worse."

As he was begging for alms one day, along came a man who decided to be the merchant's "partner," and insisted that whatever money the merchant got would become his.

And so when Elijah encountered the merchant one day and heard about what was happening, Elijah repeated, "Things could be far worse," and left him.

Well, one day, the man who had become his partner died. What could the merchant do but carry him to a cemetery? But the body was heavy and, oh, it began to smell. The merchant could not beg for charity while carrying the body. He thought that this would be the end of him, too.

One rabbi suggested that the seven vanities of Qoheleth were the seven ages that humans pass through in life. As babies, we are treated like royalty, our every need met immediately. As toddlers, we seem like pigs, always getting into places we shouldn't. As youngsters, we skip about like young goats. In our late teens, we dress up like show horses and attempt to attract the opposite sex. Once married we work like beasts of burden. When children come along, we go after food and provisions for them with the tenacity of dogs. When we are old we become bent over like apes. Seeing this, the Preacher says that all is vanity. (Ecclesiastes Rabbah 1.2 [1])

When he got to the cemetery, he buried the body and then walked along the country road. He sat on a rock and cried. Elijah happened by and asked him what was wrong.

The merchant replied, "I see now what you meant by the expression 'Things could be far worse.' There seems to be no end to this bad luck. And so what's the use of complaining?"

When Elijah and the merchant returned to the city, Elijah blessed him and wished him well.

From that time, things began to improve for the merchant, and soon he had his business and his livelihood again. And he never again complained. (Peninnah Schram)*

*Originally published as "Things Could Be Far Worse" in Tales of Elijah the Prophet, by Peninnah Schram.

World Enough and Time

There is a time appropriate to all the contradictory experiences of life.

The Story

For everything its season, and for every activity under heaven its time:
a time to be born and a time to die;
a time to plant and a time to uproot;
a time to kill and a time to heal;
a time to break down and a time to build up;
a time to weep and a time to laugh;
a time for mourning and a time for dancing;
a time to scatter stones and a time to gather them;
a time to embrace and a time to abstain from embracing;
a time to seek and a time to lose;
a time to keep an a time to discard;
a time to tear and a time to mend;
a time for silence and a time for speech;
a time to love and a time to hate;
a time for war and a time for peace.
What profit has the worker from his labour? I have seen the task that God has given to mortals to keep them occupied. He has made everything to suit its time; moreover he has given mankind a sense of past and future, but no comprehension of God's work from beginning to end. I know that there is nothing good for anyone except to be happy and live the best life he can while he is alive. Indeed, that everyone should eat and drink and enjoy himself, in return for all his labours, is a gift of God.

Comments on the Story

The sage has reconvened his little group at the corner of the market square. They are solidly with him now, and he can sense their expectation that his uncommon wisdom will shatter yet another icon of everyday life. The Solomon persona has succeeded beautifully; the students, all of whom are masters of their own households, can see in the weariness of the old king their own much-compromised dreams of glory. "Good work," he thought to himself. "They must lose their provincial attitudes. They think like villagers; their biggest concerns are getting the best stall in the square and plotting revenge on their neighbor who cheated them ten years ago. Fools! The world out there is run by Greeks who can reflect on the cosmos and its conundrums. Of course, their gods are ridiculous, but their philosophers' power of thought, the range of their interest, their elegant manner of expression—it is all superior, vastly superior. So I will do what I can."

The sage begins his lesson with a poem so beautiful it makes his hearers' hearts ache. This poem remains one of the best-known passages in the entire Hebrew Bible. Its subject is "the times," and by this the Speaker meant something particular. Traditionally in Israel the word translated "time" did not signify an abstract concept but specific, meaningful events. Continuous time is a succession of individual "times." So the Speaker begins by reminding them that everything that is has its own moment for occurring, and that these times, or "seasons" are appropriate for each. Here the expression "everything there is" *(hakol)* is paired with a word translated "activity," which may be either work or desire. The seasons of all there is are just like the times of what people are concerned with, their activities in the broadest sense. The Speaker refers to the wisdom of the ages, not only in Israel but also in the ancient Near East, which took as its charter the discernment of proper times for certain actions and words. Human life was ruled by the necessity of appropriate times, on the analogy of the bird that knows when to migrate (Jer. 8:7); trees that know when to send out their fruit (Job 5:26); or even babies, who know the proper time to be born (Hos. 13:13).

The Speaker now begins to enumerate his vision of the completeness of human life, like the composer of proverbs who wrote, "Three things there are which are stately in their stride" (Prov. 30:29). He begins with birth and death—the limits of life. There is planting and uprooting—crops, gardens, the growth and movement of families—breaking down and building up—of houses and city gates, of the arrogant and the humble. There is a time to scatter stones and to gather them together; perhaps the hearers remember a field that was ruined when someone spread stones in the soil; perhaps they themselves cleared ground for cultivation. Perhaps they think of their physical love of their wives, as later rabbis did when they read this passage. The simple pairs resound with associations, each of which adds validity to the list.

With every pair of opposites, therefore, the Speaker tells of all the life held between the two extremes. He does not judge these events or even present some as negative and others as positive. They simply occur, each in its turn, at the appropriate time and at the right season. The pendulum swings back and forth, and all these things have a place in the life of an individual—she will live and die, she will laugh and mourn, she will embrace and hold herself back, she will seek and accept loss, she will love and hate, wage war and make peace. If she is wise, she will observe these proper times and do what is required of her. Like the farmer in Isaiah 28:23-29, who knows the proper times to plow the earth, sow the seed, and thresh his harvest, the wise person gains knowledge of the times from God (both the fact that there are proper times and the basics of what each time might be) and uses native intelligence to figure out the rest. So the young man and woman must use their knowledge of the times to provide for their households, as we learn in Proverbs 27:23-27 and 31:10-31.

But this is not the end of the story, as we might suspect from our past experience with the Speaker. After invoking this grand tradition of appropriate times and activities for his hearers, he brings them back to his theme with an abrupt change of style. All these doings (the word used for "worker" refers to the activities for which there is a right time and season) are merely labors from which one gets no profit. After skillfully holding moral judgment at bay during the poem itself, the Speaker now interprets it for his listeners. His rhetorical question returns us to the utter skepticism that we saw in the previous reading. There is nothing of value to be realized and preserved from the observation of the right times. Traditional wisdom has failed to provide for the existential needs of the people. The remaining two verses of our text now account for the Speaker's new perspective on the wisdom doctrine of the times.

The reasons for the failure are plentiful. First, there is the fact that it is worthless in itself; the Speaker has already mentioned in the preceding verses. Here he makes it a matter of observation: "I have seen that God has given humankind business just to keep us busy." But God has done more than this. The "everything that is" that he has made (the Speaker avoids the word *created*) is beautiful (not "good") when it is supposed to happen (lit. "in its time"). That we know. And God has given human beings awareness of those times ("put past and present in their minds"—the RSV "eternity" is inadequate and the REB/NRSV "a sense of past and future" is better but still too vague). But God has also made it so that humankind cannot find out what God is actually doing from first to last. That is, we are stuck with our awareness that things are meant to happen at certain times, and that this is good. However, we cannot find out, despite our desire to know, what God means by it and whether it all adds up to anything for us. Therefore, we can never say with any certainty about a particular event, "It was God's will that this take place."

The Speaker's students must have been brought low by this point. Not only are all our activities dull and pointless, but now he says that God thwarts our desire to know and do his will on earth! Sadly one of them acknowledged that this may be true, recalling the pain he had caused the man whose son was murdered by thieves when he piously pronounced his death "God's will." Another recalled last season's drought and the pitiful harvest; another, the mysterious disease that killed his family's cow. God does indeed obscure his path, and even the wise cannot find it out, try as they may.

But out of this remembrance of tragedy the Speaker reaches in and pulls out his treasure: life in the present. Perhaps you do not have an advantage, a profit from your labors, but you do have a portion *(heleq)* or a share from God. No, it is not the piece of land that was passed from generation to generation within a family—or even the land in general, as they were accustomed to think. The real good (not beauty) for human beings is to accept happiness and prosperity when it comes (if it does). The fact that your labors provide you with enough

113

to eat and drink and enjoy yourself is itself a gift from God. It is not something you control yourself.

The fruits of this recognition will appear in later portions of the book, when the Speaker returns to the theme and embellishes it for his listeners. In 3:22 they are counseled to enjoy their work; in 5:18, to enjoy wealth while they have it, and think less of the passing years; in 8:15, there is a repetition of 3:12. But the best account of the Speaker's counsel is in 9:7-10, and in these words lies the consolation of the sage. Do not be overcast or bitter in life, he says, because God has already accepted what you have done. Take a proper interest in your food, your clothing, and a few luxuries in life. Live with someone whom you truly love, and whatever it is you do for a living, give all your strength to it. This is your profit and your reward; there is nothing else. No looking past the grave to eternal life; we don't count that. Let your awareness of death concentrate your efforts to live fully, and do not burden yourself with anything too complicated. Nothing is that important. Like the famous poem "Desiderata," these words are a quiet testimony to balance and equilibrium in life. Perhaps it is not surprising that the Speaker should build a great thicket of skepticism around them for protection.

We might stop to wonder what the Speaker's students eventually thought of his teachings, beyond the powerful affirmation of preserving them for future generations. Fortunately, we have not one but two editorial comments on the Speaker's life as a sage, and they are found in the end of the book. In 12:9, we hear a retrospective of the sage's life and work. He was a teacher, but he also tried to educate the people in general and contributed his own research in the field by composing and collecting proverbs. The next verse, although it is difficult to translate clearly, seems to praise the Speaker for his originality. His sayings are "the work of one shepherd"—that is, not diluted by being a collection drawn from many sources. The second comment, however, is less indulgent of the Speaker. The wise soul who added this formal ending to the book clearly meant to discourage the wholesale production of volumes of individual wisdom. He ends with a note of piety that clashes with the bracing honesty of the Speaker's own words. Where the Speaker may have been lax on discipline, the editor feels free to compensate. Such is the fate of any writer or storyteller who pretends wisdom!

Retelling the Story

For everything its season, and for every activity under heaven its time. (Eccles. 3:1)

Life is puzzling. Sometimes good things seem to happen to undeserving people, while bad things happen to righteous people.

I remember that as a youngster I often asked my father why this was so. He would respond by saying: "We cannot know everything.

"All of life is like a circle, but a person can see only an arc and not the com-

> One sage taught that the phrase about a time to die and a time to be born suggested that we should be as free of evil deeds on the day we die as we were on the day we were born. *(Sefer Ha-Aggadah* 583.79)

plete circle. We often do not know the reasons for what happens, but while a person must ask questions, he should not ask too many questions."

In a certain town, there lived a God-fearing and good man, Reb Shmuel ben Yosef. He trusted God and accepted whatever happened to him and to his family—most of the time. Sometimes, though, he was puzzled by the things that happened to his people. "Why should such a good woman as our neighbor Sarah is—why should she suffer the death of her only child, while others who do not practice charity and perform good deeds—why do they enjoy large families?" he would ask of God, not to speak ill of people, Heaven forbid, but only out of a sense of confusion.

Once, he saw a wealthy family become poor. "How cruel that this family will be without all the things they are accustomed to," he thought. "Why did God do this?"

Other things troubled Reb Shmuel as well. Day after day, as he looked around, he would ask again and again, "Why?" and "How?"

And he began to ask more and more often. "Ribono shel Olam, Creator of the Universe," he would call out, "help me understand Your ways. I know Your miracles are everywhere. But I am beginning to see only the despair, and I am perplexed by what I see. If only I could meet Elijah the Prophet. Maybe then I could begin to understand and see once again your daily miracles." Reb Shmuel fasted and prayed that he might see Elijah the Prophet.

> The sages said that the specific information that was hidden from humans in God's creation was the day that a person would die. This was a blessing, they said, because then we would keep planting our crops and making our plans and if we don't benefit from the harvest, then someone else will be blessed by our work. If we knew when we would die, we would be too likely to simply stop living and, in a sense, die before our deaths. At the same time we would be depriving others of blessings. *(Sefer Ha-Aggadah* 584.86)

One day, as he was walking in an open field, a stranger approached him and said, "I am Elijah. What would you ask of me?"

Reb Shmuel answered, "I need to see the wonders that you perform in the world, for my world is dark, and I do not understand much of what goes on around me."

And Elijah said, "When you see what I do, you will certainly not understand my actions. Then I will have to explain them to you, which will take time . . . ."

"No, no, I promise I will not take up your time or ask you to trouble yourself with me," Reb Shmuel assured him. "I will just come along with you to observe—to witness your miracles. That is all."

"Very well," said Elijah, "but remember—if you ask for any explanations, I shall leave at once."

Reb Shmuel had no choice but to agree to this condition.

He began to walk with Elijah until they came to a small cottage where there lived a poor man and his wife. They had very little and owned only one cow, but they received the strangers with a warm welcome. Placing whatever food they had on the table, they invited the two men to sit and eat. All evening, they discussed some points of law, and the hosts were delighted to have such learned men in their home.

In the morning, as they were about to leave, Elijah gave a signal and the cow, this couple's only cow, suddenly died. As Reb Shmuel and Elijah continued on their way, Reb Shmuel muttered to himself in anger, "This is some repayment for kindness! That these kind people, who welcomed us so graciously to their home, should be so repaid!" Unable to hold back his deepening confusion, he turned to Elijah and pleaded, "Why? Why did you cause their cow to die?"

Elijah kept walking as he replied, "Have you forgotten what I asked of you? You must not ask for an explanation no matter what I do—or else I will leave."

Reb Shmuel wanted to argue and ask, "But where are your miracles that save lives or help the poor?" Instead, he said nothing more and continued to walk behind Elijah.

That evening, they came to the mansion of a wealthy man. They knocked on the door. The master of the house sent his servant to bring the two men to the place where the servants slept. But since they were offered no food, not even a piece of bread, they went to bed hungry. In the morning, as they were leaving, Elijah noticed a tree near the house that had been uprooted by a storm.

Elijah passed by the tree, nodded, and the tree righted itself, with its roots deeper in the ground than before.

When Reb Shmuel saw this, he was even more puzzled. He thought, "To restore his tree! Why should a stingy man receive such a reward from Elijah?" But he said nothing to Elijah. He hoped he would understand in some way, perhaps by some sign or word from Elijah.

All day long they walked, until they came to a synagogue in another town. When they entered, they found that the seats were made of gold and silver. The people sat in their seats, but no one rushed to welcome them or to give either one his seat, and not even one person invited them to his home for dinner, as was customary when strangers came to a town.

Since no one asked them home for dinner, Elijah and Reb Shmuel remained in the synagogue all night, sleeping on the hard benches in the back. The next morning, as Elijah stood by the door, he said to all the people, "May you all become leaders!"

Again Reb Shmuel did not know what to make of all this.

The next evening, they stopped at a small community where everyone was extremely poor. But the people welcomed the two travelers and asked them to stay with them. Everyone began to bring food to the synagogue, and soon there was a wonderful feast with plenty of wine and food. When they left in the morning, Elijah said to the people, "May God bless you with only one leader."

Reb Shmuel waited until they were on the road, and then he turned to Elijah and cried out, "No more! No more! I cannot continue to see such injustices done. Forgive me, but even though I know you will leave me, please tell me what you have been doing. I do not understand any of this. It appears to me that you are doing the opposite of what the people deserve." And Reb Shmuel wept.

Elijah replied, "My friend, listen carefully. Do you remember the poor couple whose cow died? The wife was destined to die that very day, so I pleaded with God to accept the cow's death in place of the woman's.

"When we were at the home of the greedy rich man, I straightened the tree that had fallen over. Had I not done that, the man would have found the hidden treasure that lies in the ground under the tree's roots.

"When I wished the wealthy but selfish people in the synagogue to have many leaders, that may have sounded like a good thing. But it was a curse, because any group that has too many leaders cannot agree on anything and can never make any decisions.

"Therefore, when I wished for the poor but hospitable community to have only one leader, that was a blessing, for it is said, 'It is better to have one wise man rule a city than a group of fools.' "

One sage suggested that the statement that God had made everything suit its time meant that each vocation was suitable to the ones who worked at it, offering them not only money but delight as well. *(Sefer Ha-Aggadah* 608.379)

Before Elijah departed, he said to Reb Shmuel, "I want to give you some advice that will be useful to you, my friend. Whenever you see a wicked person who is prospering, keep in mind that his wickedness will ultimately work against him. And if you see a righteous person enduring hardships, remember that perhaps that person is being saved from something worse. Do not doubt these things any longer. One cannot always understand all of God's ways."

Elijah departed. And Reb Shmuel returned to his home, seeing once again the wonders and miracles in the world.

And so may we all. *(Peninnah Schram)**

*Originally published as "Elijah's Mysterious Ways" in *Tales of Elijah the Prophet,* by Peninnah Schram. This story is found in the eleventh-century Hebrew collection of folktales, *Hibbur Yafe Mehayeshua,* which was modeled on a widely known Arabic genre of "tales of relief after adversity and stress."

IV. Ecclesiasticus (The Wisdom of Jesus ben Sirach):

A Narrative Introduction

An ancient Chinese curse says: "May you live in interesting times!" It is true that important events eclipse worthy individuals, obscuring their achievements and denying them the fame that they deserve in history. However, Jesus ben Eleazer ben Sirach, or simply Sirach, the author of a collection of his own wisdom and instruction that dates from the second century before Christ (c.190 B.C.E.), seems to have escaped this fate. He lived in a highly significant period of Jewish history, and he was a person of substantial accomplishment whose writing has earned a prize beyond all others: a place in the deuterocanonical literature of the Bible.*

Although most of the books in the Bible, including the Apocrypha, are anonymous, in the Wisdom of Sirach we have a book in the modern sense, including an identifiable author, Jesus (Yeshua) grandson of Sirach, and a translator/publisher, his own grandson (he humbly chose to conceal his own name), who in 132 B.C.E. translated the work from the original Hebrew into Greek for Jews who were living in Egypt. Considering its sheer length (over

---

*The Wisdom of Jesus ben Sirach was not included in the Jewish canon because, among other possible reasons, the early Christians were already using the Greek version found in the Septuagint, thereby lessening its status. The original Hebrew version of the book was not recopied and was therefore thought to be lost. The church, on the other hand, continued to use Sirach extensively as a book of ethics and ultimately included it in the Old Testament canon; hence its traditional name, "Ecclesiasticus," which means "Of the Church." Subsequent copies of the Greek text in the church included additions such as glosses and readers' comments on the text. Portions of the original Hebrew text have been recovered in modern times. As the REB translators note, the Greek version of the text was used as the basis for their translation, and the Hebrew text was consulted for help with difficult readings. Sirach became part of the Apocrypha on account of the Reformers, who modeled their canon on the shorter Jewish list. Those who wish to read the book through will find that verse numbers are not in proper sequence. This is because Christian additions to the Greek version of the text were removed in the RSV and most subsequent modern English versions long after versification was added to the first English translations of the Greek text (16th century). For a synopsis of the textual history of Sirach, see M. Gilbert, "Wisdom Literature," in *Jewish Writings of the Second Temple Period*, ed. M. E. Stone, Compendia Rerum Iudaicarum ad Novum Testamentum 2.2 (Philadelphia: Fortress Press, 1984), pp. 290-92.

fifty chapters) and the range and depth of its insight, the Wisdom of Ben Sirach qualifies its author both as a master of wisdom and as an exceptionally diligent person. As a sage he stood in a tradition of Israelite intellectuals, and he points out in his book that he studied and meditated on them constantly. As the head of a school *(beit ha-midrash)*, his religion went hand in hand with his instruction and his personal values. His writings also show the influence of the thought and rhetoric of the Hellenistic (Greek) culture, which began to appear on the scene after Alexander's conquest around 330 B.C.E.. Sirach, therefore, studied the classics of his own time, including Theognis, Homer, the stoics, and various other philosophical works, and he refers favorably to travel and consultation with foreign rulers. As a member of the Jewish intellectual elite, he may have occupied many different roles, including scribe, priest, and headmaster.

The effort to synthesize Jewish tradition and Hellenistic culture was the chief social and religious issue of the time. Because Jews from most levels of society experienced this struggle (as did all ethnic peoples in the empire to one degree or another), compromise between the two took a variety of forms, from full assimilation with Hellenistic culture and values, to a rigid insistence that the Jewish law be followed to the letter, even if it meant cultural and political isolation.

But one dynamic in Palestine would never change. This region was a corridor that connected Asia Minor with the African continent, particularly Egypt. The land of the Jews was always subject to military domination from one side or the other. In Sirach's time, Palestine was the battleground for the struggle between the descendents of two of Alexander's generals (the Diadochoi), Ptolemy I Lagi and Seleucus I. These warring factions were in fact two distinct ethnic groups, the Greco-Egyptians (the Ptolemies) and the Greco-Syrians (the Seleucids). Sirach himself lived under Ptolemaic rule in Palestine, which was relatively calm and uneventful. The Seleucids gained control over Palestine after the Battle of Panium (Cesarea Phillipi in New Testament times) in 198 B.C.E. and immediately set about to win more territory. Although initially friendly toward the Jewish population, during the 170s, the Seleucid kings eventually imposed heavy taxes on them and even raided Temple treasuries to finance military campaigns against the Romans and the Ptolemies. At the same time the Jewish high priests, religious rulers in Jerusalem who also collected tax money from their constituents for the Egyptians, were growing increasingly corrupt, forcing a showdown between the leading priestly families. In 167, one Seleucid king, Antiochus Epiphanes IV, gave a decree unifying all ethnic peoples under one imperial banner, in effect outlawing Judaism.

But the decisive blow was the desecration of the Temple in Jerusalem. In the Holy of Holies, where no non-Jew had ever stood, Antiochus built an altar to Zeus, patron god of the dynasty. The Jewish reaction to these acts was seismic.

Stories about it can be found in 1 Maccabees, whose principle theme is the Maccabean revolt and Hasmonean dynasty (the last, brief period of Jewish sovereignty in Palestine before the founding of the State of Israel in 1948).

Thus Sirach lived, worked, and wrote on the edge of crisis in Jerusalem. His book can be studied as a record of how one extremely gifted individual used the wisdom tradition to mediate between his desire to serve God faithfully by observing Jewish traditions, which removed one from the mainstream, and his desire to live peacefully and well with one's rulers, who held the key to physical survival. His story can be discerned in autobiographical sections of this book (24:30-34; 33:16-18; 39:12-15), and his concerns are reflected in the instruction itself.

Sirach's book also highlights a new role for the intellectual tradition in Israel. In Sirach, for the first time in the Wisdom writings, Israel's religious traditions are not only mentioned but deeply connected to the enterprise of wisdom. By this time, Israel's traditions have now become Tradition, which is encapsulated in one word: Law (Torah). In Sirach, Wisdom carries Torah, which is not just the Law, nor even the entire canon of Law, Prophets, and Writings (see the Preface), but the religious soul of Judaism as it is lived out every day.

Sirach, therefore, uses wisdom to help Jews practice the Torah in a Hellenistic society. This means that a significant dialogue takes place in Sirach between the authority of the Torah and the authority of a sage. Sirach reveres the law and advocates obedience to it, but he also expects his counsels to be taken seriously as spiritual discipline. His grandson characterized it this way: "My grandfather Jesus . . . was moved to compile a book of his own on the themes of learning and wisdom, in order that, with this further help, scholars might make greater progress in their studies by living as the law directs" (Ecclus.:Preface). To a later generation, Sirach's own instruction was almost— but not quite—a practical form of the Torah.

How did Sirach himself see his role as sage in relation to wisdom and Torah? In three ways. First, in his instructions, Sirach mixed religious questions with issues of ethics. He did this so well that *instruction* is almost an incorrect term for his writing. Scholars have argued that a homiletical model, parenesis, fits his sayings better. The old wisdom expression "The fear of the Lord is the beginning of wisdom" took on new life as Sirach applied it directly to context after context. For example, in two of our readings Sirach links the doctrine of retribution with admonitions against pride (10:12-18) and for justice for the oppressed, especially in the courts. Second, Sirach saw himself as an agent of God's Spirit as a writer and composer of instruction. This made his authority equal to that of the priest or the prophet—and indeed he has been mistaken for both. In one autobiographical section, Sirach compares the wisdom that flows through him (24:30; see also v. 33) to the wisdom that flows from the Torah (24:23). In another of our readings (27:4-7), Sirach's instructions about the testing of character appear in a series of discourses on sin. There is nothing explicitly religious about his language or the insight itself, but its authority is presumed by Sirach himself. Finally, Sirach took the bold step of revamping the mythology of Wisdom as goddess to locate her specifically in Jerusalem at the Temple. Wisdom itself was a possession of the Jews. He made this theological statement the core of his writing, putting it literally at the center of his book (chap. 24).

Despite the focus on the figure of Jesus ben Sirach ben Eleazar as a composer of wisdom, it would be impossible to write a biography of him. Based on his writing, scholars cannot agree whether he was a layman or a priest, a schoolmaster or an administrator, a local bureaucrat or an itinerant judge. But there is one advantage to all the role confusion: It highlights the possible social roles of the sage, including the vital transition to scribe—a perspective that the other wisdom books do not afford. The foundation for all these roles is, for Sirach, the figure of the ideal sage, which is not so much a question of the occupation of a wise man as it is a question of an individual's character, piety, and study of the Scriptures, plus the vital commodity of leisure time to be concerned with these things (see Ecclus. 38:24–39:11). The wise man, therefore, is contrasted with the craftsman, whose skills and dedication are respectfully described. But the sage, who studies the wisdom tradition and travels to foreign lands to meet rulers' demand for counsel (39:1-4), is capable of higher things than the craftsman, no matter how skilled. If the sage is truly superior, he will be a composer of wisdom and will acknowledge that its source is the Lord. Then he can expect widespread praise and admiration, and die knowing that his fame will outlive him (vv. 5-11). Sirach believed he was one of these superior sages, whose knowledge would serve coming generations.

Sirach invites students to his school (51:23), which has the distinction of being the first actual reference to a place of instruction in the wisdom literature. He addresses his listeners as sons and expects them to make the necessary sacrifices to learn from him. They must not only accept the discipline of wisdom, but find the money for tuition, "a large amount of silver" (51:28). Sirach's instructions also indicate that he could have held the post of a scribe at some point in his career. In Ptolemaic times, the scribe was a government administrator, usually at a high level (that is, not a clerk), who supervised the workings of government, keeping statistics and records, and overseeing fiscal transactions (John G. Gammie, "The Sage in Sirach." In *The Sage in Israel and the Ancient Near East,* eds. Leo G. Perdue and John G. Gammie [Winona Lake: Eisenbrausn, 1990], 367). We see this function in Ecclesiasticus 10:1-5, the portrayals of a wise judge, a wise king, and a wise scribe (read "scribe" instead of "legislator" in v. 5). The sage might have held a secular position at the court or in a court of law, and studied the Torah in his spare time as a religious obligation. But even this does not rule out having students to teach at the same time; it does lessen the chance that Sirach could lead an entire school, however.

Let us say, then, that Sirach was a Jewish layman from a priestly family, who at one time had been summoned to Egypt to be a member of a Ptolemaic tribunal, which judged cases referred to it by the local leader of the district. There he had a chance to observe and learn about human nature on a broader scale, and he even did a little extra travel on the side (34:11-12). It was a real highlight of his career. Eventually he returned to Jerusalem, where he founded a traditional Jewish school and took in students (his competitor would have been the local *paideia,* or Hellenistic school). Sirach did not become a philosopher, but remained firmly planted within the Jewish reflective tradition, eventually collecting his compositions, including sayings, instructions, hymns, and special writings, such as the Praise of the Fathers (Ecclus. 44–50), which was based on the Greek rhetorical form of encomium. He was happily married (his praise of the good wife is traditional, but Sirach seems to infuse it with sincerity), but was far more comfortable raising sons than daughters because of his great investment in scholarship, which was not directed toward women. In fact, he shows special anxiety about raising daughters (42:9-14). Sirach was traditional in his sentiments about women, slaves, and the poor, none of whom would he ever consider his peers. In both Jewish and Greek social hierarchies, these persons were of negligible worth in themselves but were valued in terms of their usefulness and the moral and religious obligations they imposed on others. Although Sirach's misogyny cannot be excused or allowed to justify such attitudes in the present, it is not sufficient cause to dismiss his thinking on other topics.

Sirach marks a turning point in the Wisdom literature of Israel in many ways. Although the book is considered "deuterocanonical" and somewhat less significant than those works enclosed within the biblical canon proper, its insights still make an important claim on us. The wisdom of Jesus ben Sirach is unique in that it offers us the pleasure of encountering a real, historical sage who self-consciously passed on the traditions of the fathers and understood the religious nature of his calling as a wise man.

Rooting Out Arrogance

God places the meek and humble in positions of power, and puts the powerful of this world in their place.

The Story

The beginning of pride is to forsake the Lord, when the human heart revolts against its Maker; as its beginning is sin, so persistence in it brings on a deluge of depravity.
Therefore the Lord inflicts signal punishments on the proud
and brings them to utter disaster.
The Lord overturns the thrones of princes
and installs the meek in their place.
The Lord uproots nations
   and plants the humble in their place.
The Lord lays waste the territory of nations,
destroying them to the very foundations of the earth;
some he shrivels away to nothing,
so that all memory of them vanishes from the earth.
Pride was not the Creator's design for man
nor violent anger for those born of woman.

Comments on the Story

This passage is part of a larger subgroup of instructions on the topic of pride (6:18–14:19). Sirach demonstrates the need for getting rid of the attitude of arrogance or pride by attaching it to some of the most important theological themes in the Wisdom tradition: the fear of the Lord, retribution, and wisdom and creation. Arrogance is not just an annoying personality trait. It is the negation of wisdom and contrary to the Creator's will for human beings, both as individuals and as entire nations. This little poem warns students that pride starts out small but ends up causing total disaster, for God will punish it all the way down to the ground upon which the arrogant stand.

The statement "The beginning of pride is to forsake the Lord" is a negative version of the familiar sentence in Proverbs: "The fear of the LORD is the beginning of wisdom." This is a classic statement of Wisdom theology. The fear of the Lord is a common enough concept in ancient Israel, meaning basically obedience to God and a desire to know God's will (rather than fearfulness of divine judgment, for example). Joining "the fear of the Lord" and "the beginning of wisdom" is the new thing, and we see it in Proverbs (1:7; 9:10;

15:33), Psalms (111:10), and Job (28:28). The sentence implies that to be obedient to God (or committed to God) is a prerequisite of wisdom. The quest for wisdom must be based on a secure foundation; this is knowledge of God and understanding of self in that light. Sirach and Proverbs agree on this point about the correct foundation of the human quest for wisdom. Sirach equates the fear of the Lord with wisdom (1:11-20) and with obedience to the Torah (1:26; 6:37).

Sirach's triad of the fear of the Lord, Torah, and Wisdom underlines the divine source of wisdom. God gives wisdom and knowledge, and human beings cannot claim to be the source of it themselves. The fear of the Lord is traditionally joined with humility, which is not to be confused with shame or lack of self-respect (see Ecclus. 41:16–42:8). Humility is a knowledge of one's own abilities and limitations as a mortal being, and then acting appropriately to one's place. Because all things have their opposite (33:14-15), the counterpart of humility is pride or arrogance (Gr. *huperthania*).

The beginning of a lifetime of pride, therefore, is based on forsaking God, which means rebellion against the Creator. This has overtones of the original sin in Genesis 3, when the first human couple defied God and were punished. After the first offense against God, however, comes a life that is "a deluge of depravity," possibly a reference to the human evil that brought on God's sending of the flood in Genesis 5–6. Once established on human pride rather than humility before God, the resulting lifetime will be filled with wrongdoing. So a religious offense becomes the basis for ethical disaster; one existential decision carries many smaller practical decisions in its train. In this way Torah is merged with wisdom under the authority of God.

God will, therefore, punish the proud in unmistakable ("signal") ways. Here is Sirach's statement of divine retribution, rooted in the reflections of the older teachers as well as the priests and prophets of Israel. What you reap is what you sow; the wicked will be punished and the righteous rewarded. Sirach reaffirms the traditional view of God's will to give humankind its just desserts, despite the refutations of this doctrine offered by Job and Ecclesiastes. His basic position on this question is stated clearly in 39:12-35: "From the beginning good was created for the good, and evil for sinners" (v. 25) and

> All that the Lord has made is good,
> and he supplies every need as it arises.
> Let no one say, 'This is less good than that,'
> for all things prove good at their proper time. (vv. 33-34)

The retribution Sirach envisions for the proud is a kind of poetic justice that is found in many hymns in the Bible, including Psalms 37, 49, 113, the Song of Hannah (1 Sam. 2:1-10), and the Magnificat (Luke 1:46-55). The very ones who were oppressed by the proud will take their places. The proud will not only be deposed from their high places, but they will be obliterated through space and time as well, rooted out so that there is no trace left of their presence on earth and so that no one even remembers who they were. For Sirach, who did not believe in resurrection as did the later Pharisees, this was total annihilation.

In fact, it amounts to a kind of "uncreation" in which the arrogant, or the "self-made," are unmade by their true Maker. Because in their arrogance they have usurped God's role as Creator, God will show mastery by working that role in reverse to punish them. Sirach can end this vision of terror for the arrogant with the simple statement that pride was not part of the Creator's plan for his creatures, or indeed the violent anger that proceeds from it. Sirach's vision of the full effects of human pride would have motivated his students to redouble their dedication to learning the Torah and to training rigorously for government service; taken as general instruction, it would have spoken effectively to those not born to a high rank in society, but who aspired nonetheless to offer their services in responsible positions.

Retelling the Story

The beginning of pride is to forsake the Lord,
when the human heart revolts against its Maker;
as its beginning is sin,
so persistence in it brings on a deluge of depravity.
(Ecclus. 10:12-13a)

Cain was just such a person as this passage describes. He was marked to protect him from being killed, but that does not mean that he escaped punishment. The rabbis suggest at least seven possibilities for the sign of Cain: the rising sun, so that the animals that stalked the night would not devour him; leprosy, which assured he would not be killed because no other human being would approach him; a dog to defend him; a horn on his forehead so he would be too frightening to approach; a punishment that would serve as a warning to others who killed; a punishment to warn people to turn from their wicked ways; or he was allowed to live until the time of the flood. Others suggest one additional possibility: The Sabbath came and saved Cain from the worst punishment. (Ginzberg, V, 141, note 28)

See that empty church building over there? Well, that used to be a thriving congregation some years back. People would flock to it because of the good-looking young preacher who started it. Oh, he was just as bright as he could be and could quote the Bible chapter and verse. His sermons were so popular after a while that the people started taping them and selling them. He even had a television program going for a while there. I hear he won some awards for his preaching from big preacher magazines, but I don't know for sure, since I don't read that sort of thing. But I did hear him a couple of times at community services, and he did put words together better than just about anybody that I ever heard.

From the start it was that preacher's church. A few people started meeting in the preacher's house; then they built the building over to the side there for their worship services; then when they grew out of that one they built the big sanctuary. There was a time that over a thousand people would come to services there of a Sunday. The young preacher did everything for the church. He would be there first thing in the morning, and I would look out my front window here late at night and the light would still be on in his office. He preached revivals just about every week, and Saturdays he would go places teaching other preachers how to do things the way he did.

I guess you could say he was a success. He certainly was a hit with the community. All ages, too. Young people flocked around him, and the elderly folks treated him like he was the son they wished they had. The only people that seemed to do without his attention were his wife and children. I didn't really know them, but I've seen them on Sunday dressed to beat the band coming into church. You've never seen a nicer family, but I reckon I saw just about as much of them as he did. I guess he was just too important to be cooped up at home. I never heard whether they liked or didn't like his being gone all the time, but I had my suspicions as to how they felt.

Well, the church just kept getting bigger, and he kept dressing better and driving bigger, finer cars on his pastoral visits and revivals and teaching trips. I know what you're thinking. You're thinking he ran off with the organist or the church secretary or something like that, but it didn't happen that way. No, he was just so successful that he couldn't stand to be cooped up in this little place. He was hired as the senior pastor of a big city church that had its own school connected with it. I don't blame him for going; nobody did. Before long everybody in town knew that they had doubled the salary he got here, had a big parsonage in a nice new neighborhood, and an even nicer car to drive. There was even talk about a membership to the country club and stock options and such, but I don't know anything about that sort of thing.

When he left they gave him a big going away party and a real nice "money tree" to get his family on its way. After that, though, things seemed to just fall apart for the church here. The preacher had done everything for so long that the people didn't seem to know how to do anything for themselves. They had nobody to depend on, not even God. They didn't even know how to lock and unlock the place. They even talked about naming the church after that first preacher. When they didn't, they lost a lot of people to other churches where there were other up-and-coming preachers. A few even moved to the town where their first preacher had gone. They just couldn't stand to listen to anybody else on Sunday. When they finally got a new preacher here, half the folks didn't like him because he wasn't exactly like their first preacher, so they left. Soon those who were left were bickering over who had done more to get the church started or to get it through its time without a preacher, and a group left to start their own church down next to the new subdivision.

> Leprosy was thought to be the punishment of choice for those who were greedy and sought to acquire great wealth. Thus it was said to be so for Cain, Job, and King Uzziah. In addition, Naaman was said to have become leprous due to his arrogance concerning his great accomplishments. (Ginzberg, V, 141, note 28 and III, 214)

Those who were left couldn't keep up with the building, so they sold it to one of those new groups that I had never heard of. So the church that preacher built singlehandedly is gone, but I hear that preacher has gone to an even bigger church now and is doing right well. I never hear about his family though, but I think about them a lot.

(Michael Williams)

The Choice to Obey

God wants all people to follow the Commandments but gives us the choice of whether to observe them or not.

The Story

If you choose, you can observe the commandments; you can keep faith if you are so minded. He has set before you fire and water: reach out and make you choice. Mortals are offered life or death: whichever they prefer will be given them. For great is the wisdom of the Lord; he is mighty in power, all-seeing; his eyes are on those who fear him; no human action escapes his notice. He has commanded no one to be impious; to none has he given licence to sin.

Comments on the Story

Like the previous reading, this passage is part of a larger discourse, 15:11-20, on the subject of human freedom and God's will. Sirach addresses his instruction on this point to those who excuse themselves of sin by saying, "The Lord is to blame for my going astray." Apart from the question of what the Lord is to blame for, we will immediately wonder, "Where did you go astray?" Given the context in which Sirach wrote, there is a strong possibility that the person who would make such a statement is defending himself or herself against an accusation of breaking religious law. Since God is the ultimate source of religious law, the speaker is accusing God of giving Israel a Torah that is too difficult (complicated, inconvenient, old-fashioned, etc.) to follow. Young people might especially be prone to make this case to their elders. Sirach suspects that behind their self-justification is the "love of vice" (15:13), but that is not the main thrust of his argument.

His first point is that human beings were created with free will (Heb. *yeser*, that which is formed [in the mind]; i.e., imagination or purpose). His students would remember that God issued commandments to the first human couple, which they deliberately decided to break. Like the original couple, all human beings are free. But Sirach links the power to choose with "observing the commandments" and "keeping the faith," making the point that human freedom also encompasses the ability to carry out the demands of the law. Your choice to obey the commandments is an either/or proposition, like fire or water, life or death. Choose life, he says, as did the writer of Deuteronomy (30:15-20).

This passage about freedom and personal responsibility should be set against Sirach's statement that God has predetermined events and destinies, for example 39:32-34:

> I have been convinced of all this from the beginning;
> I have thought it over and left it in writing:
> all that the Lord has made is good,
> and he supplies every need as it arises.
> Let no one say, 'This is less good than that,'
> for all things prove good at their proper time.

The Speaker, too, recognized that God made everything beautiful in its time, but denied that human beings had access to which times were right for which things. Now Sirach claims that God has determined that everything is good in its proper time but also that human beings are free to either sin or obey the commandments.

Strictly speaking, these two statements are conflicting. Israelite tradition also remembered those who seemed fated to evildoing, such as Saul in his mad pursuit of David, or self-destruction, such as Samson with his foolish attachment to Philistine women. There were, of course, traditions of innocent sufferers (such as Job) and tragic figures (such as Hagar, Jepthah's daughter, and David's daughter Tamar). But Sirach refuses to concede this point. In our text, he merely wants to make it clear that the tradition, which emphasizes God's demand for obedience to covenantal law, circumscribes the choices down to two: life and death. Furthermore, the existential nature of this choice overshadows the theoretical contradictions that are inevitable if these two principles are brought together too closely.

On the whole, however, Sirach is making another point in this text. He is arguing that a person's decision to observe the commandments confers on him or her the ability to keep them, thereby keeping the faith. In other words, there is no measurable gap between the desire to fulfill the law and the ability to do so. Neither God nor human nature nor the law itself prevents a person from being obedient if he or she truly wishes to be. Deuteronomy, a book on which Israel's Wisdom tradition had already made its mark, makes this same point in 30:11-14:

This commandment that I lay on you today is not too difficult for you or beyond your reach. It is not in the heavens, that you should say, 'Who will go up to the heavens for us to fetch it and tell it to us, so that we can keep it?' Nor is it beyond the sea, that you should say, 'Who will cross the sea for us to fetch it and tell it to us, so that we can keep it?' It is a thing very near to you, on your lips and in your heart ready to be kept.

Obviously, Sirach was conservative with regard to Torah. He advocated obedience to the law and decried those who set aside or attempted to compromise its demands (2:12; 33:2-3; 41:8). At the same time, Sirach shows a preference for some aspects of the law over others, such as the parts that show Yahweh's sovereignty, goodness, and compassion—and those parts that demonstrate Israel's high ethical standards.

Sirach also makes the point that according to Jewish religious belief, human beings discover the ethical dimension of life by embracing religious values and being obedient to Yahweh, the source and authority of all goodness on earth. The Stoics, and other Greek moral philosophers—Sirach's main competitors— taught that the ethical behavior of the wise person transcended the appropriate behavior of the fool solely on the basis of rationality; that is, the wise individual understood why a thing was right or wrong. Jewish moral thought was based on the character and deeds of Yahweh, who had covenanted with his people and commanded ethical behavior as their obligation. In Deuteronomy, obedience to the law is a sign to other nations of Israel's wisdom (Deut. 4:6). In Sirach's time, obedience to the law was still a signal to other nations.

Sirach reminds the inheritors of the tradition that Yahweh's eye is all-seeing, that it is turned on the humble with compassion and consolation, but on the wicked with a terrible scrutiny that registered all their sins and prepared a judgment against them (Ps. 33:18, which Sirach quotes here; see also Job 22:12-20; Ps. 113:4-7; Isa. 59:1-4; Ecclus. 23:19). The concept of retribution lurks behind every discussion of individual responsibility, enforcing the demand for accountability with the threat of punishment or reward.

Taken in its entirety, this passage shows Sirach acting not so much as a sage but as someone responsible for reinforcing the religious loyalties of his fellow Jews. As a counselor/pastor, he must deliver the message of God's demand for justice faithfully. The other message, that everything God makes is good in its proper time, softens the harshness of this considerably. But Sirach makes no effort to resolve these tensions directly. Sirach saw himself as responsible for teaching the tradition, not for providing an apology for it. We might see this as a wise strategem; by not retreating to a defensive position with respect to the tradition, he no doubt made far greater headway with young scoffers of the religious law.

Retelling the Story

> [God] has set before you fire and water:
> reach out and make your choice.
> Mortals are offered life or death:
> whichever they prefer will be given them.
> (Ecclus. 15:16-17)

Once there was a king who wanted to do what he wanted to do and didn't like for anyone to get in his way or disagree with his desire to do it. His every

131

wish was someone else's command. Whatever he wanted he got or had one of his loyal soldiers get for him. No one in his court or kingdom liked him, but everyone feared him.

This same king was also terribly afraid of dying. From childhood he had developed an uncontrollable fear of either burning to death or drowning. His castle was some distance inland, far from any body of water. Even so, the king took only sponge baths from a basin, which he ordered to be held behind him and at no time should it ever be placed in his sight. He drank no water, only fruit juices, and those through straws that were designed to curve around in such a manner that he was never to see the glass from which he drank. While his terror was reserved for water alone, all liquids made him nervous.

Fire was even more carefully controlled in his castle. His was the first building in the realm to employ a rude furnace. Bricks were heated, and air passed across the heated bricks and into his rooms. But because the furnace was so primitive the rooms were always cold. His food was cooked in a separate part of the castle, and by the time it arrived at his table it was moderately warm at best, but certainly not hot. Since lamps of any kind were a problem for him, the king walked about only during daylight hours and spent the hours of darkness curled up in his bed.

> The rabbis say that it is not enough to keep God's commandments. It is important that we do so with the right attitude. If Reuben had known how his timid attempt to save his brother Joseph would be recorded in history, he would have put his brother on his back and taken him bodily to their father. Or if Boaz had known how his gift of grain to Ruth and Naomi would appear in the story, he would have given them one of the calves he had been feeding and saving for a celebration. When we follow God's commandments with delight, we follow them to the utmost. *(Leviticus Rabbah 34.8)*

One day an old woman arrived at the castle gate and asked to see the king. When he refused, as she knew he would, the woman sent word that she could show him the secret to possessing two rare gifts that the king would never possess otherwise. He granted her an audience. When she arrived she told him a story, "Once there was a thief who broke into houses and took only the costume jewelry and left the diamonds, silver, and gold. He would steal an old coat but leave behind the expensive fur hanging next to it. When he opened a purse he would take the copper coins and leave the gold coins behind. What would you say of such a thief?"

The king answered without hesitation, "He is such a fool that he should give up thievery altogether, for it is much more effort than it is worth to him."

"Just so, Your Majesty," the woman continued, "you pilfer worthless items

A farmer forgot some of his grain and left it in the field. This meant that the poor could come along and glean the grain. When the farmer remembered his mistake, he told his family that they would make a burnt offering to God. His son didn't understand and asked why his father was praising God for the loss of profit that the grain represented. His father answered that God commanded that any grain forgotten in the field was to be left there for the poor. If he had left it there on purpose it would have been charity and he might have wanted to claim credit for it. Since he had forgotten it, he had simply unconsciously been following one of God's commandments. For that he would give credit to God. *(Sefer Ha-Aggadah 461.543)*

from throughout your realm yet leave the most precious ones behind."

"Are you suggesting that I am like the foolish thief?" the king inquired in decidedly sinister tones.

"Not at all, Sire. But if I could show you the two precious gifts you neglect, will you allow your subjects to keep the little property they can still call their own?"

"I will," was his only reply.

"The two great gifts of God that you have foolishly ignored are fire and water," the woman began.

"No," cried the king, "these are God's great dangers."

The woman replied with a voice as calm as a placid lake, "Each great gift has another side, which is its great danger. True, fire can destroy, but it can also warm the cold nights. And water can drown and flood, but it can also soothe a weary body in a bath as well as clean from it the dust of many duties."

The king looked incredulous, "But how can one choose the gift over the danger?"

"You must make that choice, Your Majesty. That is where wisdom enters the picture." As the old woman spoke, she removed from a bag she carried a small candle with a heating stand, a small teapot, and two cups. The king and the old woman sat and drank tea.

After that day the king was much nicer to be around, the rooms in the castle were warmed by fireplaces and baths, and hot meals and tea were the order of the day. The king lived to a ripe old age and died by neither fire nor water. Some even said that by the end of his days he had become wise. *(Michael Williams)*

Lady Wisdom Finds a Home

Wisdom, who was present at the creation, comes to dwell in Jerusalem.

The Story

Hear the praise of wisdom from her own mouth, as she speaks with pride among her people, before the assembly of the Most High and in the presence of the heavenly host: "I am the word spoken by the Most HIgh; it was I who covered the earth like a mist. My dwelling-place was in high heaven; my throne was in a pillar of cloud. Alone I made a circuit of the sky and traversed the depths of the abyss. The waves of the sea, the whole earth, every people and nation were under my sway. Among them all I sought where I might come to rest: in whose territory was I to settle? Then the Creator of all things laid a command on me; he who created me decreed where I should dwell. He said, 'Make your home in Jacob; enter on your heritage in Israel.' Before time began he created me, and until the end of time I shall endure. In the sacred tent I ministered in his presence, and thus I came to be established in Zion. He settled me in the city he loved and gave me authority in Jerusalem. I took root among the people whom the Lord had honoured by choosing them to be his own portion.

Comments on the Story

The twenty-fourth chapter of Ecclesiasticus stands between two great poles in this book. The first is the opening description of Lady Wisdom as a creation of God and her relationship to the fear of the Lord in 1:1-20, which is the process by which human beings show their desire to know and obey the will of God. The other pole is at the book's conclusion. Sirach's explicit claim to his authorship of the book in 50:27-29 crowns his attempts to explain his relationship to wisdom. In order to prevent any misunderstanding of his motives for doing so, Sirach describes his own relationship to Lady Wisdom and the Law.

From the standpoint of the entire book of the Wisdom of Jesus ben Sirach, chapter 24 is crucial. It divides the book in half (perhaps literally in the original Hebrew version; scholars have called the authenticity of chapters 39 and 51 into question), and it is one of the high points of the theology of the book. Now that the familiar Hymn to the Fathers, chapters 44–50 ("Let us now praise famous men, the fathers of our people in their generations . . . "), is no longer included in the common lectionary, this is the most significant portion of Ecclesiasticus that the church will hear in the years to come.

Once again, we hear only a portion of this hymn, which extends to verse 22; the conclusion of the chapter, in which Sirach describes his role as a teacher of Wisdom/Torah, is also necessary to look at if we want to see what Sirach has accomplished with this poem.

The first section (vv. 1-22) is written in a formal style well known to religious persons in the Greco-Egyptian world. It is an *aretology,* in which a divine being, usually a goddess, praises herself, tells her worshipers what names she may be addressed by, and describes her willingness to help human supplicants. Sirach therefore takes the figure of Lady Wisdom from Proverbs 8 and adapts it to this literary style. Sirach can thus take the figure of Lady Wisdom and put in her own mouth the point he wants to make about wisdom and its relationship with Yahweh and Israel.

She begins her story in the assembly of the hosts of heaven. Here Sirach is making reference to the mythology of a heavenly royal court where Yahweh sat as sovereign, determining the fate of the earth, while his hosts, the sons of God, paraded around him. This is traditional imagery found, among other places, in the story of the prophet Micaiah ben Imlah (1 Kings 22:19-23) and in the prologue to Job (chaps. 1–2), where God and Satan decide on a wager concerning Job's righteousness. Not much later than Sirach, the apocalyptic writer of Daniel would use this image to talk about the judgment of God at the end time. In this poem, it is significant that Wisdom's confession about her creation is not made before human beings, but before God and his host only; human beings can "hear" Wisdom's testimony only in a different setting and in concrete form.

Wisdom's language is, therefore, highly metaphorical, but it is not random. The images she chooses are allusions to Scripture and give an encapsulated version of the narrative of Torah: She was the word of God (Gen. 1); she was the mist that watered the earth before creation (Gen. 2:4); her throne was the pillar of cloud (Exod. 13:21-22). She wandered alone everywhere, but had dominion over every people; like Israel, she looked for a place to call her own. Like Israel again, she received one by the command of Yahweh.

Now she moves through Israel's shrines to Jerusalem itself. She was in the tent of meeting; established in Jerusalem (2 Sam. 6); had authority in Jerusalem (Solomon?).

So she came to rest in Israel, which was the special, covenanted people. Our reading ends here, but Wisdom's progress from heaven to earth is not yet complete. From verses 13-17 Wisdom takes root throughout Israel (the geography indicates the four compass points in Israel and Judah), and particularly in the Temple worship in Jerusalem (the spices and plants mentioned are associated with the oil of anointing and other aspects of formal worship of Yahweh). She then beckons to the next generation, as Lady Wisdom did in Proverbs, promising to satisfy their appetites with the choicest food and drink.

But at the end of this aretology comes something extremely interesting: Sirach himself now offers an interpretation of the hymn. All of this—the whole sweep of Lady Wisdom's speech—"is the book of the covenant of God Most High, the law laid on us by Moses, a possession for the assemblies of Jacob." Wisdom infuses the Torah to the extent that wisdom is identified with the Torah. This is the concrete form in which wisdom can be approached and appropriated by mortal beings on earth; in this way, they can actually hear in their own assemblies what Lady Wisdom confessed in the heavenly assembly. Wisdom is not abstract or mythological; it is the practical ethics of living given by God in the covenant at Sinai. Wisdom, claims Sirach, is like the great waters of the earth, which spread life and blessing for humankind.

Now Sirach ventures a word about his own role. He was in touch with these mighty waters, but only as a small conduit into a "pleasure garden" by which he probably meant his own school. But, he claims poetically, wisdom inspired him prophetically to expand his horizons and to partake of wisdom's own universality. Sirach's wisdom, a gift from God by virtue of his study of the Torah, overflowed its banks and sought its true level. This learning is supposed to attract foreigners and last until future generations.

Wisdom's hymn to herself, therefore, helps students to see the dynamic power of the Torah that they study. It is not a dry, dusty scroll from ancient days that they have opened; it is the moving spirit that travels through the narratives; it is the fountain of life that flows out into the life of all students, giving their lives order and sense. Its power is beyond human fathoming, but like the primal seas themselves, Wisdom is answerable to God.

Retelling the Story

> I took root among the people whom
> the Lord had honoured
> by choosing them to be his own portion.
> (Ecclus. 24:12)

Sophie had never had a home. From the time she was born she had been traded from relative to relative, none of them wanting to keep her for long. Her father had been killed in one of the many wars that had swept across her homeland over the centuries. Her mother had died a short time after Sophie was born. Although she had family in the form of aunts, uncles, and cousins, and although she had lived in many houses, Sophie had never had a home.

Then one day she was sent, without anyone asking her opinion of the move, to live with her mother's mother. She was a woman with steel gray hair and

A certain Joshua ben Gamla is credited with bringing education to Jerusalem. Before his time, fathers were expected to teach their children Torah. If a child had no father, then that child received no instruction. Even when there were others who taught Torah only those children with fathers were taken to Jerusalem to study. Finally, there were teachers who taught adolescents sixteen or older, but often the unruly ones quit school or were sent away. It was Joshua ben Gamla, the rabbis say, who began schools in each locality for children age six and above. (Sefer Ha-Aggadah 416-417.141)

glasses with gold earpieces and a gold nosepiece but no rims, only glass. She wore cotton print dresses and an apron, and she lived in a white frame farmhouse far from anyone. It was the house where Sophie's mother had lived when she was Sophie's age.

Sophie was not sure that she was going to like this new living arrangement. There were no other children her age. There was plenty to keep her busy, though. There were two cows to be fed and milked and chickens to feed and eggs to gather. Sophie's grandmother taught her to milk and feed and gather the eggs.

During the long evenings after the work was done, Sophie would sit and talk with her new guardian. In truth, the conversation was more like an interrogation, with Sophie asking the questions and the grandmother answering them as best she could.

S: "What was my mother like when she was my age?"

G: "A lot like you, full of questions."

S: "Did you live here when you were a little girl?"

G: "Yes, and I can remember my grandmother, your great-great-grandmother.

S: "Do you remember when I was born?"

G: "Of course I do; I was there helping the midwife bring you into the world."

S: "Do I look like my mother?"

G: "Some, but mostly you just look like yourself."

S: "Is this your home?"

G: "Yes it is, and I hope you will consider it your home, too."

So, Sophie spent her evenings talking with her grandmother. The days had plenty of chores to fill them, but when she had some time to spare, Sophie would go to a special place she had found. Past the barn and the chicken coop there was a small stream lined with trees. One particular tree that stood above and very near the stream had three trunks growing out of its stump of tangled roots. These three trunks emerged in such a fashion that they made a seat at the point where they parted. Sophie would sit on that seat in the cool shade and listen to the music that the water made as it flowed from wherever it came from toward wherever it was going. She was like that water, she thought, her life flowing from her dead parents toward some great unknown, but the thought didn't frighten her. In fact, sitting between the trunks listening and thinking felt like she imagined home would feel. She called the tree her thinking place and went there as often as she could.

One night after many months she was sitting, talking to her grandmother and told her about her thinking place. This time her grandmother asked the questions.

G: "What do you think about?"

S: "All kinds of things—like what I will be when I grow up."

G: "Perhaps you will be a wise woman when you grow up and think many thoughts that will benefit people around the world. Have you decided what you would like to be?"

S: "A teacher, I think."

G: "You will make a good one. What else do you think about?"

S: "Home—what it's like to have one, a real home where people want you there when you are there and wish you were there when you are away."

G: "That's exactly the way I feel about you. Do you think this might be home?"

S: "With you here and the tree, yes, I think it is."

(Michael Williams)

One rabbi suggested that the reason Jerusalem was destroyed was that young children were no longer being taught Torah. The phrasing of Jeremiah that God's wrath would be poured out in the street meant that the children were running about in the streets instead of being taught in their classrooms. *(Sefer Ha-Aggadah* 419-420.166)

The Test of Speech

Words spoken in the heat of argument are a true reflection of a person's character.

The Story

Shake a sieve, and the rubbish remains; start an argument, and a man's faults show up. As the work of a potter is tested in the kiln, so a man is tried in debate. As a tree's fruit reveals the skill of the grower, so the expression of a man's thoughts reveals his character. Do not praise a man till you hear him in argument, for that is the test.

Comments on the Story

Although all of Sirach's advice aims at helping students develop the ability to distinguish between true and false, good and evil, life and death, justice and oppression, sin and righteousness, the little passage before us here announces itself as something special. There are few true tests of a person's inner quality; in most cases, those who seek wisdom must rely on the borrowed insights of teachers subjected to personal experience (meaning making mistakes and learning from them). Little things can mean a lot, as Sirach knew ("You can tell a person by his appearance and recognize good sense at first sight. His clothes, the way he laughs, his gait—these reveal his character" [19:29]). Or one may observe the manner of a person's death, for in the end that, according to Sirach, is what will show the true quality of a person's life (11:27). "Call no one happy before he dies, for not until death is a person known for what he is" (11:28).

But these tests are not foolproof. Sirach was well aware that appearances do not always correspond to reality. A rumor that is widely believed may be completely false (19:4-17). A scoundrel might affect sympathy but seize advantage from it (19:26-28). Under no circumstances trust an enemy: "Even if he appears humble and cringing, keep your distance and be on your guard" (12:11). Despite this, he counsels strongly that the real test of character is a person's ability to communicate. The NEB adds a slight nuance to the text, so that it becomes communication under pressure (e.g., in an argument or debate). But this is not really necessary; the test is simply conversation.

Underlying this advice is the traditional wisdom teaching about the power of human speech to accomplish both good and evil. Good talk was related to the power of wisdom in the form of a proverb. In a practical context this was the right word spoken at the right time, the signal achievement of the wise, considered an ethical act in itself. In a religious context the human word draws its significance from the word of God, an expression of the will of God, which has ultimate power and authority to accomplish its purpose (see Ecclus. 39:17-31). In Israelite wisdom this word is, of course, identified with Lady Wisdom ("I am the word spoken by the Most High" [24:3]).

In older Israelite wisdom, which borrowed heavily from traditional Egyptian wisdom, silence was exalted as a sign of wisdom for the royal courtier. Proverbs contains many warnings against too much talk (10:19, 32; 11:12; 12:13-14, 19; 13:3; 15:23; 18:13). Sirach gets at the ambiguity of silence as a strategy for the wise in 20:5-8: One person is silent and is thought to be wise; another is silent because he actually has nothing to say. In general, Sirach has a sharp sense of the various kinds of harmful and annoying speech to avoid, such as being garrulous (9:18; 21:7), betraying confidences (13:12-13), making rash comments (14:1-2); rude speech, rumormongering, crude talk by children, unnecessary talk at parties ("When you are old, you are entitled to speak, but come to the point and do not interrupt the music"), and so forth.

Sirach's points are made with three comparisons from different aspects of life. The first comparison uses a sieve to catch "rubbish" (lit., "dung," "refuse"). Scholars have related this saying to the process of threshing wheat, which when first sifted will leave behind straw that has been matted together with ox dung. When a person talks, the "trash" in his or her mind will be obvious to everyone. The second compares a person to a pot that will break in the heat of the kiln if it is not sound (i.e, has hot air trapped in it). The third comparison is also agricultural: As the fruit on a tree shows the skill of the grower, the speech of a wise person shows the effects of training and discipline. This imagery is put on Jesus' lips in Matthew 7:16-19 and 12:33-37.

The early Christian communities shared Sirach's interest in the power of speech to either build up or tear down. The test of speech was stressed particularly in James, a second-century CE book of counsel written from a Christian perspective. There it is related to the task of teaching others about the faith, which required special care to avoid divine judgment (3:1). James also offers instruction to Christians in general that echoes our text's analogy between speech and the fruit on a tree. One who blesses God and curses his or her neighbor is as unnatural as a fig tree bearing olives, or a grape vine producing figs (3:10-12).

Retelling the Story

As a tree's fruit reveals the skill of the grower,
so the expression of a man's
thoughts reveals his character.

(Ecclus. 27:6)

The sages say that we can wrong someone by our spoken words. They give several examples: We can pretend to be interested in buying something that we have no intention of purchasing. We can direct people who are selling goods to the wrong market. We can act as Job's friends did toward those who have experienced the death of a family member or who are ill themselves. We can say to converts that they have lived in an unclean manner and thus are unworthy of studying Torah. Or we can remind them that their forebears did not follow the God of Israel. Those who use words in such harmful ways reveal the meanness of their character.
(Sefer Ha-Aggadah 657-658.186)

Once there was a rabbi who never argued. He never disputed with his students, nor did he hurl harsh words against his opponents. While most other teachers could be found arguing the fine points of the law day in and day out with anyone who would listen, he went about his days never raising his voice to correct another or to convince anyone else of his point of view. Some thought he was a very holy man; others thought he was a simpleton.

It was not the case that his disciples never needed a guiding hand. They did, as all other students need correction from time to time. Instead of railing at them, their rabbi would say simply, "You may be right in your interpretation, but have you thought of it this way?" His voice would never rise above the tones of polite conversation as he poured forth a wisdom much deeper than the student had even begun to consider. But the rabbi's reply was offered in such a gentle fashion that the student went away rethinking his own position. The rabbi would think to himself how lucky he was to have such bright students, such independent thinkers.

Sometimes rabbis from other schools of thought on the law would approach him and attempt to start an argument. After hearing what his would-be opponent had to say, the rabbi would reply, "You are a very wise teacher, and I am but dust and ashes. I, however, look at things a little differently." Then the gentle rabbi would lay out his own view on the subject at hand with such clarity that some of those coming to argue with him and prove him wrong stayed on as his disciples. The rabbi would always think after such an encounter how fortunate he was to have persons to come and share their wisdom so freely with him—and without his even asking them to.

Once a student asked the teacher why he responded to challenges without argument or dispute. Did he not think he was right in his own beliefs? "Of course, I think I am right in my beliefs, but I could be wrong. Who is right but God? Besides, even God changes his mind. He created the world, and when the project turned out like so many of mine and just didn't work at all he repented of creating all that is and brought the flood. Then, the Torah says God repented of having destroyed it as well. Am I better than God that I should never be open to change my mind? The people God sends to challenge me are the greatest gifts anyone could receive from the divine hand. If I argued against them, I would miss the wisdom they possess, just as they would miss the wisdom that God has given me to offer them. Besides, we might both be wrong; then we would have lost the chance at friendship over two wrongheaded beliefs. That, my friend, would be too great a loss."

Not only speaking but also hearing hurtful or obscene speech was to be avoided. Some sages suggested that God had attached the earlobe to the ear so that when such destructive speech should be hurled our way we could stop up our ears with the lobes. *(Sefer Ha-Aggadah* 703.157)

In his great old age the rabbi was given the holiest opportunity of his life: He went to live in Eretz Israel. He died there and was buried in its holy ground. They say a fig tree grew up from the ground above his grave, and when it bore fruit its figs were the sweetest anyone had ever tasted. *(Michael Williams)*

142

Gifts to the Lord

God shows us by example how to live a just life.

The Story

Do not offer him a bribe, for he will not accept it,
   and do not rely on an ill-gotten sacrifice.
The Lord is a judge
   who is no respecter of persons.
He has no favourites at the expense of the poor,
and he listens to the prayer of the wronged.
He never ignores the appeal of the orphan
or of the widow as she pours out her complaint.
How the tears run down the widow's cheeks,
and her cries accuse him who caused them!
To be accepted a man must serve the Lord as he requires,
and then his prayer will reach the clouds.
The prayer of the humble pierces the clouds;
before it reaches its goal there is no comfort for him.
He does not desist until the Most High intervenes,
giving the just their rights and seeing justice done.

Comments on the Story

More noticeably than the other readings from Sirach, this passage begins in the thick of Sirach's advice with a reference to a "he" who will not accept a bribe. Of course, the antecedent is God, but the momentary confusion reminds us to start, once again, at the beginning of the entire section if we want to understand this shorter segment of it. Actually, we had best begin in the first half of the book, where the themes of this extended discourse first appear. Sirach devotes individual sections of advice concerning the mercy of God to the poor, against relying on one's wealth, against repentance without reform, and advocating the fulfilling of obligations to support the Temple and give charity early in the book (chaps. 4, 7, and 11). Sirach's deliberate repetition of these topics toward the end of the book (chaps. 34–36) suggests that he was especially concerned that these points not be lost. In the later passages, he skillfuly weaves these themes together into a subtle tapestry of ideas about what constitutes acceptable sacrifice to God for the wise.

As we have seen in Proverbs, God's special protection of the poor was a traditional theme in the wisdom literature. Sirach carries this tradition forward, cataloguing the ways in which the poor might legitimately raise a complaint against one better off in society (4:1-10). This includes withholding charity that is due or insulting the dignity of the poor. God, who is the special protector of the poor, will respond to the poor person's pleas and will punish the offender. Wise persons, on the other hand, by meeting their obligations to the poor, find themselves favored by God and held in esteem in the community.

As a sign of reverence to God and love for the creator, the wise person should show respect for priests, supporting them by giving them their due in offerings of all kinds.

Another closely related theme is the proper view of money. Sirach stresses that, although one should enjoy one's wealth and not be grudging toward oneself (14:3-19), possession of wealth does not offer absolute protection from life's hardships. Well-off individuals who are wise will not assume that they are self-sufficient and, therefore, constitute a law unto themselves. Whoever trivializes God's mercy by sinning deliberately, being confident of pardon (i.e., Bonhoeffer's "cheap grace"), can expect punishment. God can work retribution slowly or quickly. Wealth accumulated without regard to ethical behavior is particularly untrustworthy "on the day of calamity" (5:1-8).

Sirach brings these overlapping themes into close connection in the larger context of this reading, a contrast between the worship of a wicked man (34:18-26) and the worship of a just man (35:1-11). The wicked person will bring a gift to God that represents the profit on oppression or crime (but priests would not accept such money, if they knew its source; see Matt. 27:6-7). Like the prophets Amos and Isaiah, Sirach sees the contradiction between unethical behavior and cultic correctness; such rank hypocrisy would surely be punished by God. To stress the point, Sirach uses a proverb with a brutal image: "To offer a sacrifice from the possessions of the poor is like killing a son before his father's eyes" (recalling the torture of King Zedekiah, recorded in 2 Kings 25:7). The wicked man who steals from the poor as good as murders them. His sacrifices are offensive to God in the extreme. Likewise, the sacrifices of the one who uses the cult to salve his conscience but has no intention of reforming his life are worthless.

The wise man, however, intensifies the efficacy of his sacrifices by obeying the law, by repaying kindnesses, by giving alms, and by performing sacrifices as the law commands. These are effective actions; God receives them and repays the gift "seven times over" (35:1-11).

Following on the description of the behavior of the wise, our reading (vv. 12-17) becomes a word of warning to the wise: Do not think that by fulfilling your obligations for charity to the poor and sacrifices in the Temple that you have purchased preferment from God. That now becomes bribery, which invokes the pattern of the wicked (34:18-26). If the wicked risk all by forgetting that God will punish evildoers, then the just risk all by misunderstanding how God rewards righteousness. One cannot gain spiritual security through wealth applied to cultic requirement. When one's motivation is thus corrupted, the sacrifice is tainted.

Naturally, the wise man has no business offering sacrifice based on the profit from oppression. But in stressing this point, Sirach seizes an opportunity to illustrate God's merciful nature toward the deserving. The poor have absolute access to God because of their total dependence on him (vv. 13-14). The wise man sees this example and realizes that he too is vulnerable and dependent upon God for mercy. Thus he becomes truly humble—and finds his way out of the dilemma of unacceptable sacrifices (vv. 18-20). The humble wise man joins the poor in praying for justice until God is moved to act against the oppression. Chapter 36, then, is such a humble prayer for deliverance from the injustice of foreign oppressors.

In this passage, Sirach shows himself to be a subtle and masterful teacher. Initially he draws his students into recognizing the plain contrast between the wicked and the just at worship. Then he presses the wise to see the internal workings of piety toward God and its resolution in external circumstances of injustice. To identify with the poor is to become truly humble; to make their cause one's own cause is the pursuit of justice. The great prophets Amos and Isaiah could only approve of the teaching of their son, ben Sirach.

Retelling the Story

> The Lord is a judge
> who is no respecter of persons.
> He has no favourites at the expense of the poor,
> and he listens to the prayer of the wronged.
> (Ecclus. 35:12b-13)

The rabbis taught that judges should not take money for deciding a dispute, but they might charge a fee for the loss of time that usually would have been taken up by their other work. An equal fee was often charged to each participant in the case. It was not only prohibited to take a bribe to let the guilty go free but to imprison an innocent person. Bribes were not allowed even for imprisoning the guilty or releasing the innocent. Justice should not go to the highest bidder.

A similar story is told about two rabbis, both of whom were named Ishmael. When someone offered them a bribe both refused and turned the case over to someone else. Still, each began to think of the advantage of this person's pleading one way or another. If they who took no bribe gave so much consideration to the one who approached them, how could a judge who took a bribe ever dream of rendering an impartial decision? *(Sefer Ha-Aggadah* 738-739.172-179)

Once there was a woman who was noted for her ability to sew and her skill in the art of cooking. She sewed fine clothes for the very wealthy, but she never neglected to make clothes for those who could only pay a little or not at all. She prepared fine dishes for those who sat in hand-carved chairs at large silver laden tables, but she never neglected to make additional food for those who had no table or those who had no place to live. Her effort was just as great in serving those who had nothing as those who had much.

As she grew older, she decided that she must begin to prepare to die. Since all she knew was sewing and cooking that would set her apart from other souls who would meet God in the hereafter, she decided to create a special cloak that would befit the Creator of the universe and a dish that would delight even a divine palate. For the last years of her life, she worked to perfect her two gifts.

By the time the woman had completed the cloak, her hands could hardly hold a needle anymore. The recipe she devised herself was burned in her memory, and it was a good thing for she had long since lost eyesight enough to read. With her last ounce of strength, she made the special dish, and then she died.

> When judges protect the rights of widows and orphans, they are acting after the example of God. It is God, after all, who is the parent to the orphan and the protector of ones who have no protection, of which group widows are only one example. Thus the judge who acts with compassion toward those who are oppressed is not only acting wisely, but in a godly fashion as well. *(Sefer Ha-Aggadah 507.33)*

She found herself walking along a road whose end she could not view even with her newly restored sight. Accompanying her were hundreds of other souls, and though they spoke languages she had never heard, she had the sense that she understood their every word. Suddenly, walking next to her, appeared an old man whose clothes were so ragged that he was almost naked. The woman thought, *How can I allow anyone to meet his Maker in such a ragged state?* So she turned to the man and offered the cloak she had made for God. He accepted it without a word of thanks and wrapped himself in the luxurious garment. *At least I still have the dish,* she assured herself.

Soon, though, she spied a woman with three young children, all of whom were crying. They were dirty and poorly clothed, and the old woman knew that they were crying from hunger. With hardly a thought she turned and offered her dish. The woman smiled, and the children jumped at the food like hungry animals.

Now I have nothing to show of the few gifts God allowed me while I was on earth. I have nothing but myself to offer, and God knows that is nothing to brag about. Before long she approached a gate where people stood interviewing those who wanted to enter. She assumed that those asking the questions were angels. One of them approached her. She started to say, "I was bringing the most beautiful, delicious gifts . . . " but the angel put his finger to her lips to shush her. Then she was motioned into the gate without a question being asked her.

She was ushered into a large hall where a banquet was in progress. The aroma from the ovens smelled familiar, and the woman was startled to notice that everyone in the huge hall was eating her dish. And as she looked around she was shocked to see that each person was wearing a cloak just like the one she had given away. The angel turned to her and said, "Welcome. Sit anywhere. The cloak and dish you made for God and gave to those in need are now reserved for you. You see, God, like you, is no respecter of persons, but one, like you, who never forgets the poor is most like God."

The woman thanked the angel and found her place at the table. *(Michael Williams)*

V. The Wisdom of Solomon:

A Narrative Introduction

The Jewish community in Alexandria, a major seaport on the Mediterranean coast in Egypt, was in turmoil. Although the city, which was only a few centuries old, had no deep roots in the region by Egyptian standards, its citizens were prosperous and devoted to the preservation of Greek culture. The Jews who lived in Alexandria had been there from the founding of the city, and they constituted the largest Diaspora community in the world. They were a powerful group.

As they saw it, their constant task was to balance their religious identity as Jews with their desire to live peacefully and well in a land not traditionally their own. When religion and society collided, which fortunately was rare, a compromise was usually sought and achieved. To help people remain observant, Jewish scholars in Alexandria translated the Scriptures into Greek (the Septuagint) and perfected a philosophical method of interpreting the texts. Although their ancient religious traditions recorded that they were once Pharaoh's slaves, this was hardly relevant to life in Egypt over a thousand years later.

Or was it? These days it seemed that their traditions were noticed more than their contributions to the city. The Greeks and Egyptians carried on their own religious practices without remark. But things were different for the Jews: The old stories and practices of Israel were being hung around their necks, and the city leaders called them aliens and strangers. Jews were citizens in Alexandria, but it looked as if this status would soon be withdrawn. Once their citizenship was gone, so were their civil rights, which included the right to own their homes. This meant that they could be expelled at any time. Slavery in Egypt was a distant nightmare, but it could recur.

In these perilous times a young man sat at his writing desk with a stack of papyrus sheets and a fresh reed pen. His plan was to write a book to encourage his fellow Jews to reaffirm their understanding of and commitment to the ideals of their faith. Like them, he had adapted his faith in response to society's demands. He was a philosopher, trained in rhetoric, cosmology, natural science, and history. He pondered his decision. His action would not appear courageous to many in his community; when the Jews were threatened with genocide in Persia, did Mordechai write a book? But the young man knew well the powerful effect from books of philosophy in the Greek world; no public debate would take place that did not show the effects of the writings of the pre-Socratic philosophers, such as Parmenides, Heraclitus, and Democritus. He knew that Plato's *Dialogues* and the writings of Aristotle had changed how people saw the world—all people, not just the Greeks. Books could indeed be revolutionary, and it was a change of thinking that his people and their leaders needed desperately. He would refer to the old stories, but only to make his philosophical points. In this way he would show that he was guided by God-given reason above all. His arguments would carry the day with the elders of the community, and his book would be copied, distributed, and discussed in neighborhood synagogues. Then it could make a difference.

The anonymous writer of the Wisdom of Solomon (or Wisdom) wrote his treatise in Greek and in the style of an exhortation. These are significant details, since they signal a conscious rejection of Hebrew, the original language of the more conservative Ben Sirach, and the use of proverbs, also the province of the old schoolmaster. At the same time, however, the content of the book is thoroughly biblical and philosophical. Writing approximately two centuries after Sirach, or sometime in the early first century C.E., the author of Wisdom chose a literary voice for his thoughts and used the persona of Solomon, the patron of Israelite wisdom, as did Ecclesiastes and the author of the Song of Songs. Resounding through its chapters are ideas drawn from Genesis and Exodus, Kings, Isaiah, and the Psalms. From the Israelite wisdom tradition, the author of Wisdom borrowed a major figure: Lady Wisdom. His relationship with her is one of unparalleled intimacy, amounting to a marriage.

The Wisdom of Solomon is commonly known as the most "Hellenistic" book in the canon, and it is certainly the most philosophical writing in the Israelite intellectual tradition. We may even say that the author was a philosopher rather than a sage, which implies a special relationship to Greek philosophy, in which a similar distinction was made between traditional practitioners of wisdom and those who followed Plato (4th century and after). The author of the Wisdom of Solomon assumes a great deal of Greek philosophical thought, particularly the academic thought following in the train of Plato, known as Middle Platonism. On particular topics, such as immortality, eschatology, the nature of wisdom (sophia), nature and the cosmos, and free will versus determinism, Wisdom does not echo Plato's thoughts but shows an awareness of platonic views. Critics have argued that the author of Wisdom wrote at the same time as Philo, the great Jewish philosopher of the first century who devised a philosophical synthesis between Judaism and platonic thought.

It is important to stress the fact that having philosophical ties with platonism does not mean a rejection of religion or an acceptance of atheism per se (although atheism itself was a logical possibility which certain philosophers discussed). On the contrary, platonic thought was itself a synthesis of Greek religious and intellectual traditions, a way for individuals to move beyond religion centered in behavior and institutions alone. Socrates, the historical person made into the hero of Plato's philosophical works, the *Dialogues,* was said to be an extremely pious person. By the time the author of Wisdom wrote, Greek and Hebrew modes of thought had been mixed and matched by Diaspora Jews for centuries. The intellectual elite maintained a universalist perspective that fostered unity of thought, even if it could not provide social or political acceptance.

Jewish writers used the Greek intellectual tradition for their own purposes, however. Platonic thought helped the author of the Wisdom of Solomon to develop a method for understanding his own religion. As a philosopher, he could ignore his heritage altogether or become a strict literalist.

Instead, he chose a more interesting strategy, asking himself a very fundamental, very platonic question: What is the highest good for human beings, and how can they attain it? The book is his attempt to answer this question by looking at Scripture, tradition, and, of course, his own experience as shaped by his philosophical training. The author of the Wisdom of Solomon is, above all, a theologian.

Along with Sirach, the Wisdom of Solomon is found in the Christian Apocrypha. The early Christian church preserved and valued the Wisdom of Solomon because here for the first time in biblical literature the concept of immortality is explicitly introduced. There are hints of this idea in other literary works of the time, including the book of Daniel (12:2-3), but the Wisdom of Solomon stresses the theme again and again as the solution to the problem of evil. Why do the wicked prosper? Wisdom's answer is that their good fortune is only an illusion. In the end, they will be exposed in their wickedness and the righteous who were sacrificed will live forever. His solution is, therefore, that God will judge everyone according to his or her deeds after death, a divine promise of ultimate justice to console the righteous, even if their suffering cannot be lifted at the time.

The common lectionary contains eight readings from the Wisdom of Solomon, though they are often alternate readings. Such a broad sampling of texts from this book gives us an opportunity to see the book's complete argument, an unusual opportunity for Israelite wisdom literature. In the Wisdom of Solomon we have the thoughts of a young man whom we will call the philosopher. The philosopher has dedicated himself to the single-minded pursuit of wisdom from an Israelite perspective, which is one in which Yahweh is acknowledged as the source of wisdom. As we will see in the stories, his vision builds a conceptual world out of the raw material of Israelite story and legend.

It is illuminated by Israel's, and now Judaism's, hope for justice and peace in the broadest sense—that is, for the whole world.

The storyteller on a first reading of the text might not sense immediately opportunities for communicating the message offered by the philosopher. The comments below will attempt to put flesh and bones on the philosopher's persona, and then to show how the philosopher is appealing to very familiar stories, metaphors, and images in the biblical tradition. In a sense, the philosopher gives the storyteller the moral of a story, and we must recreate the plot by imagining the setting of the sources that are used by the philosopher.

The Garden of Eden and Eternal Life

God, the Sovereign of all that is, is God of creation, not death.

The Story

For God did not make death, and takes no pleasure in the destruction of any living thing; he created all things that they might have being. The creative forces of the world make for life; there is no deadly poison in them. Death has no sovereignty on earth, for justice is immortal. . . . But God created man imperishable, and made him the image of his own eternal self; it was the devil's spite that brought death into the world, and the experience of it is reserved for those who take his side.

Comments on the Story

The philosopher opens his book (1:1) with an exhortation to the leaders of the world: "Love justice . . . set your mind upon the Lord in the right way, and seek him in singleness of heart!" The writer's concern with the ethics of kings is a frame around this section. Its conclusion may be found in 6:1-16, which is also included in the lectionary. Scholars have called attention to the connections between this device and Hellenistic "kingship treatises," which were being written by Greek and Roman philosophers during the same time. Kingship treatises included lists of the virtues to be required for proper leadership and for the instruction of young men who were vying for administrative posts. According to Hellenistic philosophers, the ideal ruler was a combination of sage and politician, a philosopher-king. The perfect Israelite analog for this figure is, of course, King Solomon. The entire section from 1:1–6:16 can be seen as an extended introduction to the correct exercise of kingship. Seen in its full philosophical splendor, the question of proper government and who should lead it is the very broadest of topics.

The opening exhortation on the purity of kings also gives us a chance to see how the philosopher will use specialized vocabulary to refer to humankind, wisdom, and the deity. There is a fully developed anthropology in place before the author ever alludes to the original stories that supposedly set these patterns. His preconceived views about the nature of humankind will determine his reading of the Genesis story of creation, which is, ultimately, the subject of our reading, and a telling hint for the storyteller.

In the first section of our reading, the philosopher makes three distinct statements: (1) God did not make death; (2) the creative forces of the world also foster life; and (3) justice has eternal life. These three different entities—the creator God, derivative creative forces, and justice—offer life as the common denominator, which by its nature logically excludes death, destruction, and the reign of injustice over time.

Each of these three statements has its own background. The philosopher's first assertion, that God did not create death, is an interpretation of the stories of creation in Genesis 1–2. He bases his claim on the fact, which may be ascertained with a cursory reading of the Genesis text, that there is no description of the creation of death there. This statement is then coupled with the statement that God does not take pleasure in the destruction of living beings; the passage in Ezekiel to which this passage alludes refers not to the destruction of the living but the destruction of the wicked. Existence is now being joined to the moral quality of life. This reality is reinforced by the second statement, the idea that not only God, but also the creative forces of the world join in the affirmation of life and the exclusion of death. The notion of creative forces and the possibility that they contain deadly forces may be derived from Gnostic thought, which dealt with special "knowledge" about mystical things, particularly the escape of a transcendent being from its imprisonment in the corrupt material world, created by an inferior deity, a "demiurge." The philosopher rejects this view and asserts that creation was good from the outset. Evil is not inherent in the universe but is chosen by humankind.

The third statement about the immortality of justice has a mythological background, for death could be treated as a powerful spiritual entity in and of itself. The gods of death in the Canaanite and Greek religious traditions had times of ascendancy, such as when an individual died and was carried down to the nether regions. But the power of death was also acknowledged in religious ritual. Persephone, who ruled in the underworld, was able to punish evildoers for all time and, therefore, pious Greeks offered sacrifices to propitiate her. This idea also stands behind the claim in Revelation that death and Hades will be conquered at the final judgment (Rev. 20:14). The philosopher does not deny that death is a powerful reality, but he claims that it has no kingdom on earth, being displaced by justice, which is immortal. We will return to the idea of immortality, for it is far from clear what this word actually signifies.

These three initial statements are spliced with another, and stronger, statement about creation: God created human beings "imperishable," meaning that they would never die. This is implied, the philosopher asserts, by the fact that God, who is eternal, created the first human beings in God's own image. Once again, this is an interpretation of the creation story in Genesis. Scholars have noted that a close reading of the text actually shows that Adam and Eve were never meant to live forever. Indeed, they came close to a chance at immortality—the tree of life was near the tree of knowledge—but lost it when God punished them for eating the forbidden fruit by casting them out of the Garden of Eden (see James Barr, *The Garden of Eden and the Hope of Immortality* [Minneapolis: Fortress, 1993]). The philosopher reads Genesis to confirm his understanding of human free will, so that the human choice to sin results in death. This view finds its way into the teaching of Paul, whose simple phrase "the wages of sin is death" has deeply influenced Christian readings of the creation story.

"The devil's spite" shows the full extent of the author's reinterpretation of Genesis 2–3, for in the ancient narrative the tempter in the garden was simply a snake who was crafty, not a devil who was spiteful. The idea that the snake is actually the devil, a fallen angel, may also account for the description of the king of Tyre in Ezekiel 28, and the allusion to the fall of Lucifer from heaven ("Bright morning star,") in Isaiah 14:12-14. We can thank the philosopher in part for making the devil such a strong personality in subsequent storytelling from the Bible.

Retelling the Story

> For God did not make death, and takes no pleasure in the destruction of any living thing; he created all things that they might have being. (Wisd. of Sol. 1:13)

I got my first kitten the same year I was in Mrs. Rosemary's kindergarten class. The kitten was named Judy, and I took it to kindergarten for "pet day" the very first week that it was mine. It was soft and spotted, and everyone loved it. That was on Friday.

On Sunday afternoon we got in the car to go to my grandmother's house. As the car backed out the driveway there was a "thump" noise underneath. When we looked, Judy was dead.

Back at kindergarten I told Mrs. Rosemary, "My kitten died *for no reason!*" I cried in front of the whole class.

Mrs. Rosemary calmly gathered us together. "Boys and girls," she began, "nothing dies for no reason. If something dies it is either because it got too sick to get well, or too hurt to get well, or just too old to get well.

"If you are very careful, and very lucky, you may get to live to be too old to get well!"

Even at age five I was satisfied. Judy had simply been too hurt to get well. That explained it all!

Mrs. Rosemary's husband, Herman, was a constant presence at kindergarten.

The rabbis agreed that appearances could be deceptive. Take life and death: People walk around on the face of the earth, looking alive, but the rabbis contended that those who embraced sin as a way of life were dead, though they appeared to be alive. Those who had been buried seemed to be dead, but the rabbis taught that those who were righteous lived even though their bodies were buried. This demonstrates that God does not choose death for any individual but that we choose death when we cut ourselves off from God. (Ginzberg, V. 99, note 72)

He, according to Mrs. Rosemary, had been gassed in the war and had only one lung. He had a hole in his throat and talked with a little speaking tube. We were afraid of Herman until one day he got on his hands and knees and we all got to finger paint his bald head!

One day Mrs. Rosemary arrived at kindergarten to tell us that she would be out for a few days. Then she told us that Mr. Rosemary had died the night before. When some of us started to cry, she gathered us again and told us, "Boys and girls, nothing dies for no reason.

"If something dies it is either because it got too hurt to get well, or too sick to get well, or just too old to get well. Remember what I told you about Mr. Rosemary's one lung? He just got too sick to get well.

"Remember, if you are very careful and very lucky, you might get to live to be too old to get well." We stopped our crying.

All through the years after kindergarten, Mrs. Rosemary kept up with me. With each trip home I would be told, "Mrs. Rosemary asked about you." She continued to have small classes of kindergarteners for years and years.

Finally, on a trip home, I learned that Mrs. Rosemary had died. I went to visit her daughter to express my appreciation for my teacher and to offer a word of sympathy. But in the end, Mrs. Rosemary again took care of me.

"I'm sorry about your mother," I said to Ernestine.

Rabbi Judah taught that there were ten things that were strong. The mountains are strong, yet the iron can cut through them. Iron is strong, but the heat of a fire can melt the iron. Fire is strong, but water puts it out. Water is strong, but clouds carry it through the sky. Clouds are strong, but wind pushes them along. Wind is strong, but we can push against it with our bodies. Our bodies are strong, but fear leaves them limp. Fear is strong, but wine drives out fear. Wine is strong, but sleep will dissolve its effects. Sleep is strong, but death is stronger still. There is one thing stronger than death, however, and that is compassion. (Sefer Ha-Aggadah, 666-667.266)

"Oh, don't be sorry," she answered. "Mother probably never told you this, but she always said that nobody ever died for no reason. She always said that people died only if they were too hurt to get well, or too sick to get well, or too old to get well. And Mother was very lucky; she got to live to be too old to get well!" *(Donald Davis)*

The Persecution of the Innocent by the Wicked

The godless who persecute an innocent person will get their just desserts, and holiness will be rewarded.

The Story

But the godless by their deeds and words have asked death for his company. Thinking him their friend and pining for him, they have made a pact with him because they are fit members of his party.

They said to themselves in their deluded way: 'Our life is short and full of trouble, and when a person comes to the end there is no remedy; no one has been known to return from the grave. . . .

' . . . Let us set a trap for the just man; he stands in our way, a check to us at every turn; he girds at us as breakers of the law, and calls us traitors to our upbringing. He knows God, so he says; he styles himself "child of the Lord." He is a living condemnation of all our way of thinking. The very sight of him is an affliction to us, because his life is not like other people's, and the paths he follows are quite different. He rejects us like base coin, and avoids us and our ways as if we were filth; he says that the just die happy, and boasts that God is his father. Let us test the truth of his claim, let us see what will happen to him in the end; for if the just man is God's son, God will stretch out a hand to him and save him from the clutches of his enemies. Insult and torture are the means to put him to the test, to measure his forbearance and learn how long his patience lasts. Let us condemn him to a shameful death, for, if what he says is true, he will have a protector.'

So they argued, and how wrong they were! Blinded by their own malevolence, they failed to understand God's hidden plan; they never expected that holiness of life would have its recompense, never thought that innocence would have its reward.

Comments on the Story

This text allows us to take another look at the philosopher's view of humankind, which started with statements about the goodness of God's creation and the voluntary nature of wickedness. Death was not created; it occurred when human beings chose to associate themselves with the devil (2:24), and death is still the fate of everyone who makes this choice. Corresponding to the original duality between life and death, there are two basic

157

groups of people. At this point the philosopher is merely following the traditions of Israel's poets and wise men and women who talked about the two ways, wisdom and folly, and the people in them, the wise and the foolish, as well as the righteous and the wicked. In the Wisdom of Solomon, these two categories are explicitly combined. The wise are righteous, and the wicked are foolish. To see the difference between the two, the philosopher shows us the perspective of the wicked, and in the manner of Hellenistic diatribes, he even makes them speak.

Foolish evildoers have made a pact or covenant with death. Following the mythical allusions to death in the previous text about creation, death is now downgraded to the force of evil and destruction in life (1:16), and finally to the cessation of life in the human body (2:1). It is the simple fact of physical extinction, however, that gives the wicked their most powerful stimulus to action. Their awareness is centered on the brevity and misery of their lives; the wicked pity themselves for the trouble life causes them (cf. Job 14:1-2) and seek recompense by chasing pleasure and leaving the mess for someone else to clean up (2:9). The attitude of the wicked is crude hedonism, bearing only a superficial resemblance to the simplicity of Ecclesiastes, the moderation of Sirach, or the *carpe diem* ("seize the day") theme in Epicureanism. The wicked reason that "might makes right," which is the argument of Thrasymachus in Plato's *Republic*, and the subject of the entire dialogue entitled "Gorgias." The wicked also believe that the world has two kinds of people: the powerful and the weak. As the powerful ones, they will not miss their opportunity to tyrannize the weak.

Here our reading picks up again, though the storyteller may have already begun to think of retellings that imagine a world where powerful wicked persons are crushing the weak. The wicked resolve among themselves to set a trap for the just man (Gr. *dikaios*); to test his claim that he is God's child; and to condemn him to a shameful death. The wicked characterize the just man as one who observes the law and reminds the wicked, whether explicitly or implicitly, that they do not. He makes them feel guilty for their thinking and their way of life, and they cannot bear his condemnation. This portrait of the righteous owes a great deal to the servant songs in Second Isaiah (Isa. 42:1-4; 49:1-6; 50:4-9; 52:13–53:12). The servant of Yahweh is an innocent sufferer whose mission is to establish justice among the nations and to show God's glory on earth. The vision of the suffering servant was identified with the prophet Isaiah and with Israel as a whole, and the latter is the most likely referent. Early Christians saw in the servant songs a model for the life and death of Jesus of Nazareth. It is probably the echo of the servant songs in this passage (2:17-20) that made St. Augustine interpret it as a prediction of the passion of Christ (*City of God*, book 17).

But the philosopher adds in an editorial comment on their speech that the reasoning of the wicked has left out one crucial factor: God's mysteries ("hidden plan") in which the reward goes to those who lead holy lives. The use of this term signals that we are now moving into a discussion about life after death, which was designated as a mystery in apocalyptic literature (e.g., 1 Enoch). The wicked think that they will not be punished, but they forget that God has promised to reward the innocent even if they have been put to death by the machinations of the wicked. The philosopher has thus moved beyond the writings of the earlier sages of Israel, who believed that retribution would be carried out within the framework of a lifetime and held out no hope for redress after death. Job 14:10-12 is characteristic:

> . . . when a human being dies all his
> power vanishes;
> he expires, and where is he then?
> As the waters of a lake dwindle,
> or as a river shrinks and runs dry,
> so mortal man lies down, never to rise . . .

According to the philosopher, the mysterious region after physical death is the zone in which ultimate justice is meted out. Human beings have access to that realm only after their own death, when they, too, will be liable for their deeds. Thus the ideas of immortality operate in a context that stresses God's justice even when the wicked appear to be getting away with tormenting the innocent. This passage may be read as an answer to the question of why evil people do the terrible things they do. That is a very compelling question. But at another level, the text responds to an even better one: Will we ever see the day when the wicked are punished and the innocent restored? Yes, says the philosopher, you will see that day when your own turn comes!

Retelling the Story

> He knows God, so he says; he styles himself "child of the Lord."
> (Wisd. of Sol. 2:13)

John Andrews had been the treasurer of Christ Church for over fifty years. Every year at nomination time he would say, "Preacher, if you can find somebody else to take this job, I think that would be a good thing to do." About a week or two later he would say, "Preacher, I hope you've found somebody to be the treasurer, but if you can't find anybody, I'll still do it." For the six years that George Gordy was pastor of Christ Church, he never even tried to find anybody else to take the job.

> Moses defended the children of Israel from God's wrath after they made the gold calf. The rabbis tell that Moses reminded God that for the sake of ten righteous persons Sodom would have been saved. When challenged to name ten righteous persons, Moses could come up with only seven names. Then he added three more—Abraham, Isaac, and Jacob. Their righteousness meant that, though physically dead, they could be counted as alive. God relented and allowed the Israelites to live. (Ginzberg, III. 134)

Mr. Andrews was a saint, and everybody in town knew it except Mr. Andrews himself. He was consummately trusted not only with people's contributions to the church but with their hearts and lives as well. People knew that he spent Monday mornings in the church office counting the money and paying the bills. If they happened to need pastoral advice, they would drop by then. George Gordy had learned that if he happened to be out of the office on Monday mornings, people would get to share their troubles with Mr. Andrews, who was the very person they most trusted, the person they viewed as wisdom itself to begin with.

Every time Mr. Andrews was known to overhear someone criticizing another person, he was remembered to have simply said, "It's a good thing God didn't make ever'body all the same." That was all the gentle rebuke it took to set many people to looking more kindly at one another again.

George Gordy retired from his ministry after six years at Christ Church. His replacement was Chris Winton.

Chris Winton had just graduated at the top of his seminary class. He told George Gordy, as he looked around the pastor's study on his first visit to Christ Church, "I have more books than you have." The only way anyone even knew that Chris Winton was at the top of his seminary class was that he titled his first sermon "At the Top of God's Class."

At the first meeting of the church board, Chris Winton announced his vision for Christ Church. "New values," he called it. "Progress!" One specific suggestion was that active church offices be held by younger people and that the old people (as he called them on that occasion) be "relegated" to symbolic positions.

"Old people make mistakes," he said. "And when you're at the top of God's class, you can't make mistakes." Since Chris Winton was the preacher, Mr. Andrews took him seriously. When time came for nominations Mr. Andrews went to his preacher and said, "Preacher, if you can get anybody else to take this job, I think it would be a good thing. Sometimes it takes me two or three counts before I get the money to come out right."

By the next day, Mr. Andrews had been replaced. Now, on Monday mornings, when people stopped by the office to talk about their troubles, they found

160

their new preacher there. He talked to them a lot about being at the top of God's class, but never mentioned anything about how God might have a pretty big class.

At the end of the year the time came to make recommendations to the conference about the return of the pastor. Curtis Hammer, Chris Winton's own choice to head the Staff Relations Committee, made the report: "Reverend Winton," he began, "is surely the smartest preacher we have ever had. Why, he has more books than anybody. We all think he is as smart as any other two people put together!" Chris Winton smiled out loud!

"The trouble is," Curtis's report went on, "we only need one preacher, not two! So we think he is more needed at a larger church with greater needs. We're asking for a new preacher . . . and we'd be glad to take one who comes in at the bottom of God's class . . . like us." *(Donald Davis)*

In the tradition of the rabbis, in every human being is an inclination to do good and an inclination to do evil. God is the source of the good impulse, which also leads back to God. The evil impulse, however, is the same as Satan and the angel of death, each simply called by a different name, according to at least one rabbi. *(Sefer Ha-Aggadah 537.15)*

The Destiny of the Righteous

A righteous person is put to the test and will suffer, but have a sure hope of immortality.

The Story

But the souls of the just are in God's hand; no torment will touch them. In the eyes of the foolish they seemed to be dead; their departure was reckoned as defeat, and their going from us as disaster. But they are at peace, for though in the sight of men they may suffer punishment, they have a sure hope of immortality; and after a little chastisement they will receive great blessings, because God has tested them and found them worthy to be his. He put them to the proof like gold in a crucible, and found them acceptable like an offering burnt whole on the altar. In the hour of their judgement they will shine in glory, and will sweep over the world like sparks through stubble. They will be judges and rulers over nations and peoples, and the Lord will be their King for ever. Those who have put their trust in him will understand that he is true, and the faithful will attend upon him in love; they are his chosen, and grace and mercy will be theirs.

Comments on the Story

This story addresses one of the central mysteries of religious faith: What happens to the individual at death? Actually, it is never a question of the death of an individual, but the fate of humankind in general and "us" defined in a religious sense in particular. For the philosopher, the discussion of the fate of all humankind, which is death, is quickly converted to a discussion of the fate of the righteous versus the wicked. The question of immortality, therefore, is meaningful only in the context of God's justice and its execution among men and women.

Although the subject of this passage is immortality (Gr. *athanasia*), there are really three different patterns of "eternal life," all of which have a place in Jewish and Christian views of the afterlife. One has already been mentioned by the philosopher: God created humankind "imperishable." This suggests that at the outset, human beings were not meant to die physically but to share the eternal nature of God in their bodies, which would never grow old. As we said, the idea of death as punishment for the first sin in the Garden of Eden is part of the

162

philosopher's interpretation of the story of creation. In the philosopher's time no less than in our own, this option is hypothetical, so it can only be described in mythic terms. Thus after their transgression Adam and Eve were implicitly condemned to age and eventually die. Although this process might have been reversed with fruit from the tree of life, this path was forever closed after the pair were expelled from Eden.

The other two patterns, immortality of the soul and resurrection, are not so neatly separated. In the philosopher's time, opinion was divided on what took place after death, unless one was convinced that a person's physical death meant his or her full extinction, as the Stoics, the Epicureans, and the Sadduccean party of Judaism believed. Of those who subscribed to life after death, some regarded the soul and body as separable entities; the body might perish, but the soul, coming from God, was indestructible. Others eschewed such dualism and preferred to think of soul and body together as an indivisible unity; either way, an individual identity could survive death. By the intertestamental period, Jewish and Greek views on these topics were hopelessly intertwined, as the Wisdom of Solomon shows. The New Testament, whose pre-literary sources were being shaped at the time that the Wisdom of Solomon was written, also contains many different versions of these two patterns. For example, Jesus warns his disciples not to fear those who can kill the body but those who can kill the soul, suggesting that he believed that body and soul were separable. Jesus' own afterlife is described in no uncertain terms as a resurrection, however, so that eternal life is understood as being physical as well as spiritual. Matthew 25 vividly depicts the final judgment of the righteous and the wicked, which is given full orchestration in Revelation. Given the wide variety of opinions on this topic in early Judaism, Hellenistic thought, and the early church, it is not accurate to think of immortality of the soul as an exclusively Greek idea and resurrection a Hebrew one.

Orthodox Christian teaching inherited this vigorous hybrid of ideas. There is a tendency to combine immortality of the soul with the notion of resurrection in a sequence; once a person dies physically, his or her soul survives and goes to receive a judgment on the life that is now finished. Then on the last day, which is known only to God, the physical body will be resurrected and rejoined with the soul, and the company of heaven (and hell) will be complete. Some traditions add the idea of a final conflict between the forces of good and evil, plus the reign of Jesus Christ as God's viceroy, as in Daniel 7–12.

The philosopher begins his consideration of immortality with the status of the righteous who are now dead. Rather than the worst misfortune, death at the hands of the ungodly, the righteous who have died are in reality about to embark on a journey toward untold blessing. Here we have an important reversal of the order of existence: The death of the righteous is only an illusion, although fools take it as substantial; the immortality of the righteous is the true

163

reality, which can be seen by the wise. The death of the righteous is only a chastisement, a slight reproof or discipline from God to make certain that they were worthy for this honor. This is a traditional view that was sharpened by the thought, which was taken up and developed fully by the apocalyptic writers, that God deliberately let wicked nations prosper in their sin until the last, ultimate judgment against them.

The philosopher's vision includes the tradition that when God's final judgment takes place, the righteous saints will be rulers on earth, under the authority of God as king or emperor. It is not clear whether this includes physical resurrection, but there is nothing to rule it out. This vision of the final judgment ("great assize") recalls the apocalyptic vision in Daniel 7:22; after the arrival of the Ancient of Times in the final battle between the forces of good and evil, the tide turned: "Then judgement was pronounced in favour of the holy ones of the Most High, and the time came when the holy ones gained possession of the kingly power."

The philosopher, therefore, claims that the souls of the righteous are immortal (3:1, 4) and survive the death of their bodies. But he also sees a special time—when, he does not say—when a final judgment falls on the righteous and the wicked (3:7-9). Then the righteous will rule over a transformed world and live in companionship with God. The godless will also receive the just reward for their scheming rebellion against God (3:10). Apart from the role of Jesus Christ as the messianic viceroy, this picture is not far removed from Christian tradition concerning life after death. A final warning sets this message in perspective: The righteous can look at life and death from an eternal perspective; indeed, death itself is no barrier to their relationship with God. The wicked, however, have only cramped and limited prospects. With all present hopes, efforts, and actions for naught, with a wife and children of no account, the ungodly man has no chance to establish a name to survive his death.

Retelling the Story

The souls of the just are in God's hand; no torment will touch them. In the eyes of the foolish they seemed to be dead. . . . But they are at peace. (Wisd. of Sol. 3:1-3)

Those who are righteous let their actions speak for them, according to the sages. They do the right thing without a lot of fuss and bother. The wicked, on the other hand, make a great deal of noise about what they have done or are going to do, but never get around to doing the good. *(Sefer Ha-Aggadah 547.108)*

It was 6:24 A.M. on the digital bedside clock when the telephone rang. The day was May 10, 1973. Not more than half awake, I answered the phone to immediately recognize the voice of my cousin, my nearest "back home" relative, next to my parents and my brother.

"It's your daddy," she said. "Your mother just couldn't get him awake this morning. It must have happened in his sleep."

The message was a shock, but not a surprise. Three of my father's brothers had died of first heart attacks in the past six years, the last one, Uncle Frank, being younger than my father.

"Where's my mother?" I asked.

"She's still at the hospital," my cousin answered.

Of course, I remembered, they had taken Uncle Frank to the hospital after the rescue squad was called, even though the doctor later said that he was already dead before they got there. It all made sense.

"Tell her we'll be there just as soon as we can," I instructed my cousin, then hung up the phone.

First Uncle Harry, then Uncle Moody, then Uncle Frank, now my father. The whole world was dying.

There were phone calls to make and arrangements to put in order before we could make the three-hour trip to my parents' home. There was also a new baby to pack.

All the packing was done. It was still almost too early to make some of the calls that needed to be made. The waiting intensified the mourning. I wanted to get to my mother and brother as soon as possible.

It was nearly 8:30 before all the plans for leaving were finished. By now I was sure that my mother would be back home from the hospital and, after all, we were much later in leaving than I had led my cousin to report. I decided that, just before we got in the car to go, we should call to let the family know we were on our way.

I dialed the number, and the phone began to ring . . . then . . . my father's voice said, "Hello!" I was dumb struck. Without thinking, I said, "We just heard you were dead!"

As it turned out, it was all a gigantic mistake. Another person with my name had just moved to town. It was his father who had died and, his sister, not having his new number, had obtained ours instead from directory assistance. The mistake was so complete that she also had thought she was talking to the correct person!

We got in the car anyway and went on to my parents' house for a visit—just to be sure.

Twenty years later, my father is still alive. He was to us all, though, as dead for two hours as he could possibly be. Then the second phone call told the truth. It has left me remembering, every time I am told a friend has died, that

When the Bible says that the earth had no form and was void, it is referring to the legacy left this earth by the wicked. On the other hand, the statement "Let there be light" is a direct reference to the good that has been our heritage from the righteous. The sages also say that anyone whose heart controls them is wicked, but those who control their hearts are righteous. *(Genesis Rabbah* 2.5 and 34.1)

"with the souls of the just in God's hand," there is always a second phone call! *(Donald Davis)*

Lady Wisdom and the Parable of the Kingdom

The leader who longs for Wisdom will find that she is willing to meet you halfway.

The Story

Hear then, you kings, take this to heart; lords of the wide world, learn this lesson; give ear, you rulers of the multitude, who take pride in the myriads of your people. Your authority was bestowed on you by the Lord, your power comes from the Most High. He will probe your actions and scrutinize your intentions. Though you are servants appointed by the King, you have not been upright judges; you have not maintained the law or guided your steps by the will of God. Swiftly and terribly he will descend on you, for judgement falls relentlessly on those in high places. The lowest may find pity and forgiveness, but those in power will be called powerfully to account; for he who is Master of all is obsequious to none, and shows no deference to greatness. Small and great alike are of his making, and all are under his providence equally; but it is for those who wield authority that he reserves the sternest inquisition. To you, then, who have absolute power I speak, in hope that you may learn wisdom and not go astray; those who in holiness have kept a holy course will be accounted holy, and those who have learnt that lesson will be able to make their defence. Therefore be eager to hear me; long for my teaching, and you will learn.

Wisdom shines brightly and never fades; she is readily discerned those who love her, and by those who seek her she is found. She is quick to make herself known to all who desire knowledge of her; he who rises early in search of her will not grow weary in the quest, for he will find her seated at his door. To meditate on her is prudence in its perfect shape, and to be vigilant in her cause is the short way to freedom from care; she herself searches far and wide for those who are worthy of her, and on their daily path she appears to them with kindly intent, meeting them half-way in all their purposes.

Comments on the Story

In terms of the Wisdom of Solomon as a whole, this passage signals a transition from one major section to another. The change from a concern with the fate of the righteous and the wicked to the story of Solomon and his special

167

relationship with Lady Wisdom is very significant, and the philosopher handles it with care. These verses, therefore, constitute the conclusion of the first section proper.

The declaration to the kings of the earth in the Wisdom of Solomon 6:1-2 comes after the crescendo of divine judgment has been reached in the preceding chapters. Like a drama in which tension is built up until the final showdown between the forces of good and evil, the first section of the Wisdom of Solomon begins with the evil plots of the wicked against the good, the survival of the righteous man and the failure of the wicked, including the restoration of those who have remained faithful while carrying special burdens on earth; for example, the childless woman (3:13) is blessed with spiritual fertility, and the eunuch now receives a seat in God's temple. Finally there is a day of reckoning, which is staged for us. The just man stands with confidence, while the evil man cringes in terror. Then the wicked concede the error of their ways, and the righteous receive their reward of eternal life.

The philosopher once again ends on a mythological note. God will array himself as a warrior, as of old (see Pss. 29, 45, 74, 89) and will do battle against the forces of chaos that are in control of the earth. His weapons are lightning and hail, the ocean and rivers. God will, therefore, destroy the earth to rid it of lawlessness, as he did at the time of the great flood (Genesis 6–8).

This sequence of events is none other than an extended parable told by Solomon the King of Israel to his colleagues, the kings and princes of Rome, the latest empire. God is the real king, and his realm is heaven, from which he alone decides the fate of all beings. This has obvious implications for the rulers of the world, who will be prone to arrogance, believing that their authority is absolute. In this they are as confused as the wicked, who mistake the shadow world of everyday life as substantial in itself and cannot sense the divine meaning behind events. But the rulers of the earth need not struggle without enlightenment. To overcome their darkness, the philosopher, using the persona of Solomon, spells out the lesson they must take from his parable.

The rulers of the earth need wisdom, and Solomon stands ready to share it. Solomon's magnanimous attitude will be explained later in the text (vv. 22-25); the possession of wisdom confers virtue in a person and prohibits that person from spitefully withholding beneficial knowledge from one who needs it. Just as the philosopher makes no distinction between "research" and "teaching," so also he honors the Israelite practice of keeping the role of sage and king tied closely together—so much so that in this passage the king of Israel offers counsel like a sage to other kings.

Solomon, therefore, recalls the tradition of personifying Wisdom as a woman, which we see first in Proverbs 1–9. Like Lady Wisdom in Proverbs, Wisdom will make herself known to all who seek her, and will even meet the student at his doorstep (see Prov. 8:3). She rewards eager study ("rising early in the morning" is traditional Hebrew language for eagerness) and will accompany students on their daily paths, encouraging and promoting their projects. Unlike the depiction of Lady Wisdom in Sirach, however, there is no mention of the difficulty of mastering her discipline before her benefits are experienced (Ecclus. 6:23-31), but this may be due to the difference between accepting Wisdom's counsel as a ruler and submitting to education as a student.

The new emphasis in verses 12-16 is on the perfection of wisdom. This is a question of wisdom's proximity to God, who is increasingly described in terms of attributes raised to their ultimate power. We are now clearly in the next section of our book, and these themes will be fully developed as Solomon continues to outline his life story.

Retelling the Story

For he who is Master of all is obsequious to none, and shows no deference to greatness. (Wisd. of Sol. 6:7)

The rabbis say that the people's request for a king to rule them was appropriate, but they followed it with a statement that was not. Their reason for wanting a king was so that they could be like all the nations (non-Yahweh worshiping peoples). However, they were not to be like the other nations because, finally, their king was God. *(Sefer Ha-Aggadah 730.82)*

On April 12, 1945, President Franklin Delano Roosevelt died suddenly in Warm Springs, Georgia. Roosevelt was in the thirteenth year of a presidency that ran from the midst of the Depression through more than four years of the Second World War. Regardless of what anyone thought of his politics, Roosevelt was clearly the most powerful leader in the entire world at the time.

On April 12, 1945, Harry S. Truman had been vice-president of the United States for less than three months. With Roosevelt's death, and in the midst of the determinate full agonies of the Second World War, the former county judge from Missouri was inaugurated to replace the Harvard educated scion of wealth from Hyde Park.

This change was not the product of human plans or political process, but was the fateful result of a cerebral hemorrhage. Depending on our view of God's ownership of world history, we would call it "fate" or "an act of God" or something in between.

How did the new president react to being changed in one day from presiding officer of the senate to the center of world power?

He quoted the same Solomon whose name is preserved in this present book of wisdom. In fact, rather than claiming greatness or promising competence, Truman repeated the prayer that the ancient and wise king himself uttered when he received unasked-for power at the death of his great predecessor, King David: "Lord, give thy servant an understanding heart."

Such prayer can come only from those who know that true wisdom belongs not to us but to the one who has created us. *(Donald Davis)*

Even the dreams of foreign kings were God's doing, according to the sages. When Pharaoh dreamed, they say, it was God who created the dream and placed it in his sleeping imagination. You may remember that it was also God who gave the interpretation to Joseph. *(Genesis Rabbah 89.4)*

Wisdom's Chain of Logic

With seven arguments, Wisdom is explained.

The Story

The true beginning of wisdom is the desire to learn, and a concern for learning means love towards her; the love of her means the keeping of her laws; to keep her laws is a warrant of immortality; and immortality brings a person near to God. Thus desire for wisdom leads to a kingdom.

Comments on the Story

The philosopher ends his explanation of the parable of judgment with a polished literary summary that shows off his command of Greek rhetorical forms. The device is called *sorites,* a kind of chain syllogism used often by Greek philosophical writers to demonstrate as succinctly as possible the logical connection between key concepts or terms. The statements are linked by using the last word or phrase from one statement as the first word in the next statement. The *sorite* was not limited to the Greeks; the rabbis used *sorites,* and examples have been found in the literature of ancient Egypt, China (examples may be found in the *Analects of Confucius* and the *Tao te Ching*) and India (the *Maitri Upanishad*). Because of its compact structure and the precision it demanded, a *sorite* could also be used to show the fallacies in arguments, and many Greco-Roman schoolmasters did just that.

The philosopher has constructed a six-part chain of concepts linking wisdom with immortality and true sovereignty. There are seven ideas linked together, using synonyms at the point of each repetition. In Hebrew tradition, the number seven was the sign of completion and perfection (e.g., seven days of creation, seven years of famine and plenty in Egypt, seventy elders). Like the Pythagoreans, Hellenistic Jewish thinkers added a mystical nuance to this: The number seven became the symbol of wisdom and the light radiating from God before creation. The philosopher's choice of seven key ideas was probably deliberate, therefore. With this text, though the elegant form might be lost to the modern listener, the storyteller might experiment with a seven-part *sorite.*

The *sorite* begins with an allusion to the refrain in Proverbs 1–9: The fear of the Lord is the beginning of wisdom. The philosopher recasts this statement to make his own point, that the true (or "philosophical," as in the "true" or allegorical interpretation of the Scriptures) beginning of wisdom is the desire to learn, which means love for wisdom *(hokmah)*, which means keeping her laws.

What might these "laws" of wisdom be? Unlike Sirach, the philosopher never unequivocally identifies wisdom with Torah, nor does he mention Israel's sacrificial practices. According to the philosopher, the royal road to wisdom does not necessarily go through Israel's moral and religious law. Instead, we have the natural law of the cosmos, "the way things are" (7:17-22). It may also include the discipline that wisdom requires of each student to learn these laws. Convinced as he was that these laws constituted reality, the philosopher saw no conflict between this data and wisdom's crucial role in Israelite history. There is some ambiguity here, but it seems best to consider that wisdom's laws—whether they apply to the cosmos or to Israel's history—reflect a divinely ordained order. For the philosopher, there is no part of the cosmos or history in general that does not exhibit the will of God, that is not suffused with divine wisdom.

The pivotal move in the philosopher's *sorite* comes in verse 18: To keep her laws is the foundation (Gr. *bebaiosis*) of immortality ("warrant"). The sense is that of confirming or providing a basis for something; it can be extended to the legal sense of a warranty. To obey the laws of wisdom, which is to exhibit the philosopher's sophisticated hybrid of piety and knowledge, makes one both wise and righteous. The dualistic anthropology of righteous versus wicked now applies. When one belongs to the camp of the righteous, rather than to the wicked, one may anticipate the reward of immortality after death, as chapters 1–5 demonstrate. Immortality, of course, brings one into intimacy or friendship with God, which for a Greek might suggest the soul's return to its divine origins or for a Jew a beatific vision reserved for such worthies as Abraham, Enoch, and Elijah.

Thus, to complete the circle, the quest for knowledge is linked definitively to sovereignty. It is important to see the exercise of kingly authority in terms of the realm of God in heaven and the authority of the king on earth. Both ideas follow from the chain: One who seeks wisdom will wind up in communion with God, the King of all creation, and one who seeks wisdom will partake of the authority of God in earthly sovereignty. Like the Greco-Roman kingship tracts, the philosopher stresses that royalty derives from and is an imitation of divinity.

In the ultimate spirit of helpfulness, then, King Solomon draws out the lesson of the *sorite* (v. 21). Honoring wisdom will enable kings to rule forever, suggesting that the immortality mentioned in verse 18*b* goes hand in hand with its remembrance for all time, even after the king himself has died.

Retelling the Story

The true beginning of wisdom is the desire to learn. (Wisd. of Sol. 6:17)

On the first day of the fourth grade, my classmates and I looked at the front of the room to discover that instead of a teacher we had been assigned an antique. Our teacher was to be Miss Daisy Boyd, who was beginning her forty-second year teaching fourth grade.

Among the rabbis the pursuit of wisdom was best exemplified by the study of Torah. The fact that the creation continues to exist is due to three things: acts of compassion, worship of God, and studying the Torah. In fact, Torah study is a higher calling than that of the king. *(Sefer Ha-Aggadah* 403.1 and 9)

Our secretly whispered question to one another was, "Is she smart enough to handle us? After all, we've been going to school for three years already! We're tough!"

On that very first day, Miss Daisy proved her own toughness by catching a stray mouse in a paper towel in her bare hands, and disposing of it in the trash can, dispatched by those same God-given manual weapons! We were not about to question her abilities anymore!

Miss Daisy had very few rules. One of the few, however, was often stated to us. "Boys and girls," she would say, "you always learn more by doing something than by just hearing about it." We didn't pay much attention to that. Teachers are supposed to say things like that.

After Christmas, when we began to study the culture of ancient Greece, the usefulness of her rule became evident to us. "If she will let us *do* the Olympics (instead of just hearing about all the races) we should be able to get out of class for a week!"

We approached Miss Daisy. Bobby Jansen was the elected spokesperson. "Miss Daisy," he was giving the speech all of us had figured out, "you always say that we learn more from *doing* things than from just *hearing about them. Miss Daisy, we want to learn!* Could we do the Olympics right here at school?"

Her answer was immediate. "That's a wonderful idea, boys and girls. We must learn about the culture of ancient Greece. We'll have Olympics! Of

The Torah is compared to the fig by the sages for several reasons. First, it is sweet to study Torah. Second, because there is no pit or stone inside a fig, every bit of it can be eaten. Just so, every bit of the Torah is nourishing, and none of it useless. *(Sefer Ha-Aggadah* 405.25)

173

course, you have already read, haven't you, that in the real Olympics, athletes *ran with no clothes on?"*

It hadn't been that quiet since the day the mouse died! Miss Daisy's wisdom had separated the desire to learn from our fourth-grade incompetent version of legalistic manipulation. And we became wiser because of it! *(Donald Davis)*

The Light of Lady Wisdom

Lady Wisdom is the most radiant beauty in all of the universe!

The Story

She is the radiance that streams from everlasting light, the flawless mirror of the active power of God, and the image of his goodness. She is but one, yet can do all things; herself unchanging, she makes all things new; age after age she enters into holy souls, and makes them friends of God and prophets, for nothing is acceptable to God but the person who makes his home with wisdom. She is more beautiful than the sun, and surpasses every constellation. Compared with the light of day, she is found to excel, for day gives place to night, but against wisdom no evil can prevail. She spans the world in power from end to end, and gently orders all things.

Comments on the Story

We are now in the middle third of the Wisdom of Solomon, the section that gave the book its name and in which the philosopher makes his most challenging assertions about wisdom. Although its language is abstract, at times metaphorical, chapters 6–10 are very revealing, especially concerning the approach and values of the author. Ironically, it is when the philosopher takes on the persona of Solomon, the ancient philosopher-king of Israel, that he is being most himself.

Solomon's prayer for wisdom (see 1 Kings 3:4-15) is the setting for his observations on wisdom and the proper human attitude toward it. In the story in 1 Kings, God visits Solomon in a dream and offers him anything he wants—power, wealth, even vengeance on his enemies—but instead, Solomon humbly asks for "a heart with skill to listen, so that he may govern your people justly and distinguish good from evil." "A hearing heart" is the Hebrew equivalent of a brilliant mind. Solomon's wish is granted. The first evidence of his wisdom is sorting out the conflict between two prostitutes who are fighting over a baby (3:16-28); the following chapter describes his skill in leadership, the organization of his kingdom, and his tremendous knowledge of traditional lore. As Solomon does, the philosopher must show what wisdom means in his own era. For more than one reason, he does not want to recount the story about Israelite harlots fighting over a child. As an

175

alternative, he carefully lists the qualities of the thing he desires. That is one way in which our reading can be understood.

Another aspect of its meaning is to suggest the manner in which wisdom is attained. Like Solomon, the philosopher advocates a single-minded devotion to acquiring wisdom. Unlike Sirach, for example, whose seasoned observations on a variety of topics showed his dedication to teaching the young, the philosopher takes the posture of the life-long student. He shares wisdom not as a teacher to a student but as one seeker after wisdom to another. Thus the philosopher adds a new emphasis to the traditional story about Solomon's prayer: He recounts his passion for wisdom, whom he sought for a bride. This allows him to bypass the awkward detail recorded in the Deuteronomic history that Solomon married the daughter of Pharaoh. The list of Wisdom's qualities can also be heard as love poetry from Solomon to his true bride.

Our reading, then, is one portion of the philosopher's description of wisdom, which begins with 7:14 and concludes with 9:18. The key to this is found in 7:15-22, where the relationship between the divine gift of wisdom and the human faculty for wisdom are related; that is, God gave the philosopher the gift of understanding, and wisdom did the actual teaching. The two are so closely tied together that they are virtually indistinguishable. God is, therefore, the supreme source of wisdom—eternal and self-sufficient, like the Greek philosophers' description of their gods. Wisdom is the active principle in the world, the divine mind *(pronoia)* through which God shows care and concern for human beings, principally by ordering the world so that human beings can understand it and find their place in it.

The section describing wisdom is unapologetically Hellenistic, therefore. Like the philosophers, who criticized the crude anthropomorphism of Greek myths and instead talked about God in terms of "fitting qualities," the author of the Wisdom of Solomon attempts a more sophisticated rendering of God and his agent in the cosmos, wisdom. The Wisdom of Solomon 7:22*b*-24 is a catalogue of twenty-one characteristics of wisdom. In addition to feminine imagery for wisdom, the philosopher cites five more images to give a more complete view of the topic. Beginning with 7:25, wisdom is "a fine mist" or vapor, a breath of God; a "clear effluence" or outflowing of God; verse 26, an effulgence, or rays (Gr. *apaugasma*) of everlasting light; an unblemished mirror; and the image of his goodness. These images, piled one on top of the other, show the mystical properties of wisdom. Purer and more beautiful than the sun and stars, she is simultaneously the object of human aspirations, bringing them into intimate contact with God (like prophets and "friends of God") and the ordering principle of the cosmos. How she does this, by "[spanning] the world in power from end to end, gently [ordering] all things" is an allusion to the Stoic view that there is a continuous outward and inward

176

motion of the Spirit in the cosmos, since it is everywhere and yet holds all things together.

The universal nature of wisdom is, therefore, outlined completely. Having demonstrated his mastery of Greek doctrines and basic *theologia*, the philosopher now applies the light of reason to Israelite traditions (10:1-21).

Retelling the Story

She is the radiance that streams from everlasting light, the flawless mirror of the active power of God . . . against wisdom no evil can prevail. (Wisd. of Sol. 7:26, 30)

Throughout wisdom literature when the quality of Wisdom itself is personified, the personification is always in the feminine gender.

The sages contended that God's spirit conceived and gave birth to wisdom. This implies a feminine dimension to God even before Lady Wisdom appears on the scene. *(Exodus Rabbah 15.22)*

When I was growing up in the traditional oral culture of the Southern Appalachians, I heard many stories about wise women. The only times that men were ever called "wise" in those stories was when they were "wise *old* men!"

Thinking of these images, I cannot help thinking of my grandmother, who was, for me, a personification of wisdom. She could make any plant grow and flourish with blooms; she could graft plants and improve their fruit; she could bring a calf into the winter-heated house and force it to survive. In her entire relationship to the order of creation she was "the flawless mirror of the active power of God."

It was, perhaps, in her relationship to my grandfather that her wisdom was most profound. In a world in which men were in power, in a world in which women were totally dependent and in a subservient role in isolated mountain families, she "arranged" for herself a great deal of freedom.

She simply let him think he was in charge! Then she went right on and managed her entire life and world exactly as she saw fit. She was, everyone else saw and knew, the person whose wisdom made the world work.

The thing that makes knowledge truly beautiful and attractive is wisdom, according to the ancient sages. But there is something else, something that makes wisdom beautiful and increases its attractiveness. This is humility. Thus the truly knowledgeable are wise, and the truly wise are humble. *(Sefer Ha-Aggadah 469.4)*

Maybe there is a version of this in God's relationship to us. We think that we are so much in charge of the world. Maybe it is God's choice to simply allow us to think that—and maybe it is the assurance of our faith that God, like my grandmother, will continue to operate the world properly no matter what we do. *(Donald Davis)*

The Mighty Deeds of Wisdom

Lady Wisdom leads us to salvation in the promised land.

The Story

It was wisdom who rescued a god-fearing people, a blameless race, from a nation of oppressors; she inspired a servant of the Lord, and with his signs and wonders he defied formidable kings. She rewarded the labours of a godfearing people, she guided them on a miraculous journey, and became a covering for them by day and a blaze of stars by night. She brought them over the Red Sea, lead-ing them through its deep waters; but their enemies she engulfed, and cast them up again out of the fathomless deep. So the good despoiled the ungodly; they sang the glories of your holy name, O Lord, and with one accord praised your power, their champion; for wisdom enabled the dumb to speak, and made the tongues of infants eloquent.

Comments on the Story

In the style of an ode reminiscent of the great historical psalms (78, 105, 106, 136), the philosopher tells Israel's oldest story: the deliverance of Israel from slavery in Egypt. In doing so he adds a new twist: Instead of praising God for coming to Israel's rescue, the philosopher declares that it was Wisdom herself who was responsible for their deliverance. Given the fact that Israel's entire identity is based on these events, the relationship between God and Wisdom posited by the philosopher is clearly being forced to the test. Can the Jews of Alexandria see that their special history with Yahweh depends on the depth of their understanding of wisdom? And conversely, will their understanding of wisdom stretch to incorporate the old stories, and let them find their identity as Jews in them anew? As in the case of the historical psalms, the organization of the history and its conclusion dictates why the philosopher told the story in this particular way and no other.

The structure of the song (which begins in 10:1) relies on sets of opposites, the righteous (in each contrast, the protagonist is called *dikaios*) and the wicked. Adam is excluded from the category of the righteous, although we see Wisdom salvaging Adam from his blunder in the Garden of Eden. (It is refreshing to see that Eve is not blamed!) The wicked man who perished in fratricidal rage is clearly Cain. Next we have the generation wiped out by the

179

flood and Noah, whom Wisdom turned into a sailor despite the crudeness of his vessel. Abraham is opposed by the nation that constructed the tower of Babel (the rabbis said that he was forty-eight years old when it fell); Lot is contrasted to the residents of Sodom (and the "five cities" thereof). The poet proceeds to the conflict between Jacob and Esau, and Joseph and his detractors in Egypt. Following the philosopher's whirlwind pace, we have now reached the conclusion of the book of Genesis.

At the beginning of our storyline, the Israelites are in Egypt, which is not named but designated "a nation of oppressors." The philosopher's hatred of the Egyptians, which will emerge in force in the concluding section of the book (chaps. 11–19), is anticipated here. For the conclusion of the ode, the righteous nation of Israel is pitted against the wicked nation of Egypt. In verse 17, "the labours of a godfearing people" is probably a reference to what is called "the despoiling of the Egyptians," the curious tradition that before they fled from Egypt, the Israelites asked for and received from their neighbors gold and silver jewelry, which they took with them into the wilderness (Exod. 11:2; 12:36). In Greco-Roman times, anti-Jewish writers cited this as evidence of greed and covetousness on the part of Jews, and that their God sanctioned theft. Jewish apologetic denied this, saying the gold and silver were merely "bare wages" for slavery, which was a terrible way for a nation to treat its guests in the first place (Philo; see also Wisd. of Sol. 19:13-16).

Wisdom's activities now show her power. She enters the soul of a servant of the Lord; she is in the forces of nature which protect Israel: the pillar of cloud and the pillar of fire, which has become "a blaze of stars." She is responsible for the safe passage of Israel through the Red Sea, and she permits the fury of the sea to kill the Egyptians. In this final scene of the ode, Wisdom is virtually everywhere.

We can draw two conclusions from this outline of Israelite history. The first is that the cosmic scope of Wisdom's activity embraces, instead of excludes, Israel's salvation history. Wisdom as God's ordering intelligence cares about the fate of Israel and actively intervenes on its behalf. But it does so in a particular way. From the Torah one might get the idea that Israel's salvation was achieved only by a series of cliffhanging adventures in which God's power is proved by rescuing Israel at the last moment and in the most dramatic way. This may have encouraged a "crisis mentality" in the Philosopher's Alexandrian community. The Philosopher counters this idea by suggesting that, in reality, salvation history is the result of God's quality of compassion, which is exercised through Lady Wisdom's involvement in guiding Israel through successive stages in the progress toward righteousness as a nation. It is part of Wisdom's "gentle ordering" of all that is.

The second conclusion comes from the logic of the ode as a whole. For Israel, the recollection of communal history is never a simple reporting of past events. This particular version of communal history translates the progress of good and evil into a former time, offering a pattern for understanding the present and future time. The point of this history, and the reason it could be told no other way, is that God intends for human events to defeat the wicked and provide the righteous with occasions to praise God. Moreover no one is left out of the celebration; even infants will join in praise, being made articulate by wisdom.

Retelling the Story

Wisdom enabled the dumb to speak, and made the tongues of infants eloquent.
(Wisd. of Sol. 10:21)

When I was in junior high school there was a boy named Hallie Smathers, whom I thought was deaf and mute. Hallie never said a word, and many kids in school called him "dumb."

Gradually Hallie gravitated to living in a separate world of his own. He sat aside from the other kids in school, and as we grew older we just ceased to notice him. This continued until we were all in the ninth grade. Hallie was still there, but I would not have noticed if he had completely disappeared.

Hallie rode the bus to school from way up on Smather's Creek, where all of his family and cousins lived. The bus route to the top of the creek was uphill and then a dead end. The bus had to turn around and make a slow descent on the gravel road for about two miles to get back onto the paved road.

One Friday in the fall of the year, not long after school had started, there was a substitute driver on Hallie's route. This strange driver did not know that the old bus's brakes were insufficient for the fully loaded bus and that the bus had to creep down the grade in low gear. The turn was made at the top, and soon the full school bus was running away, far past any possibility of making it safely to the bottom.

Suddenly Hallie ran to the front of the bus, started pointing at a grove of young hemlock trees, and screamed, "Hit them pines, wild man, hit them pines!" The substitute driver caught on, steered the bus into the hemlock bushes, and the bus was safely caught to a stop. It was the first time anyone ever knew that Hallie could talk!

At least one sage taught that the Israelites were simply following religious law when they sang a song after coming safely through the sea. Those who had safely weathered a voyage at sea were supposed to recite a prayer thanking God for having mercy on the undeserving and preserving their lives. So the children of Israel were simply following the wise course, doing what they were supposed to do. (Ginzberg VI, 11, note 56)

181

When it was all over and the bus had been safely pulled out and the children delivered home, Mr. Underhill, the principal, talked with Hallie.

"We thought you couldn't talk, Hallie," he said. "Why hadn't you ever said anything before now?"

"Well," Hallie paused to think, "Before today, there wasn't ever anything that needed saying!" *(Donald Davis)*

Just as someone wishing to help a vine grow will take it out of one place and transplant it to a more fruitful place, so also God took Israel out of Egypt and placed this vine in more fertile ground. On the way they received wisdom in the form of the Torah so they might truly grow and be fruitful wherever they were planted. *(Exodus Rabbah 44.1)*

The Quality of Mercy

God is so powerful that he shows it by his lenience.

The Story

For there is no other god but you; all the world is your concern, and there is none to whom you must prove the justice of your sentence. . . . For your strength is the source of justice, and it is because you are Master of all that you are lenient to all. You show your strength when people doubt whether your power is absolute; it is when they know it and yet are insolent that you punish them. But you, with strength at your command, judge in mercy and rule us in great forbearance; for the power is yours to exercise whenever you choose.

By acts like these you taught your people that he who is just must also be kind-hearted, and you have filled your children with hope by the offer of repentance for their sins.

Comments on the Story

The third section of the Wisdom of Solomon, which is dominated by the philosopher's fulminations against the Egyptians and the Canaanites, will strike some listeners as supremely irrelevant and others as downright offensive. Why in this age of reason and enlightenment would the philosopher stoop to such a tirade? Why, indeed, after describing the universal status of wisdom? The tension between the philosopher's universal vision and his loyalty to his heritage is now finally addressed. He does this in general by setting a series of seven antitheses, or contrasts, between Israel and Egypt during the Exodus (chaps. 11–19), an elaborate apology for the destruction of the ancient Egyptians.

In the end, universalism gives way before the eternal contrast between the righteous and the wicked; the fact that Israel, a godfearing nation, has such powerful opponents is proof that God through wisdom has not wiped out godlessness and inhumanity. The philosopher, therefore, anticipates the hidden question of why God tolerates the wicked with an excursus on God's mercy (11:15–12:27). This is the context for our final opportunity to tell a story.

To make his full argument, the philosopher once again returns to first principles. On these, he insists (as the Greek philosophers would) that there is no room for compromise, no room for doubt. The philosopher, therefore, sets aside the debate form inherited from ancient Egyptian wisdom (see the *Instruction of Amenenopet* and *Onsheshonqy)*, which responded to an argument with the expression "Do not say. . . . " The debate form was used in Ecclesiastes and by Sirach, notably in a hymn (Ecclus. 39:12-35) that raises some of the same issues as the Wisdom of Solomon: "Let no one ask, 'What is this?' or 'Why is that?' In due time all such questions will be answered." The philosopher rules out debate on the nature of God, which consists of indisputable absolutes. These are absolute power (strength) and absolute love. God's strength makes him forbear and God's love gives him affection for his creation. The sum total of these things is mercy, which the philosopher will now illustrate in Israelite history.

Why, for instance, did God permit the Canaanites to live (12:3-10)? The philosopher draws on ancient traditions about the original inhabitants of the Promised Land and embellishes them freely. They were a despicable people who committed endless acts of cruelty and debauchery. But God forestalled their inevitable punishment in order to give them time to repent. With evil people, therefore, God judges little by little, correcting them so that they might mend their ways. Even so, the philosopher sneaks in some plain Middle Eastern invective; there was no hope for the Canaanites, of course, because they came from bad families, and that can't be cured! But God's mercy, being a first principle, simply cannot be questioned or debated. There are no other gods to do it, and even a human king would not presume so much. The first verse in this reading is the reason behind the preceding statement that God brooks no disagreement. The reading continues with a reprise of the absolute nature of God's qualities of strength and love. To this is added absolute freedom to exercise his power as he wishes.

These divine qualities are a part of every human being. Human beings, although they are endowed with the "imperishable spirit" *(aphtharton pneuma)* of God, and thus share his nature, may choose whether to live in accordance with this. The Canaanites' genetic predisposition to wickedness may have been the exception that proves the rule: Human beings choose whether to be evil or good, whether to accept instruction or reject it. One path means trusting God and eliminating doubt; the other means defying God to demonstrate his power against them. This passage reprises the introductory statement of the book, that fools who take liberties with God's power are shown up for what they are (1:3).

The argument about God's universalistic concern and forbearance has a special significance for Jews, therefore. Because of their loyalty to God, and the gift of wisdom they receive from him, they are enabled to see God's work as instruction for them. The grand ethic of Jewish life is the imitation of God's mercy, which makes people "humane" *(philanthropos)*.

Retelling the Story

Your strength is the source of justice. (Wisd. of Sol. 12:16)

As a young boy I did not have a bicycle. We lived where there were no good places to ride, and I was not very interested in bicycles.

One day I was visiting and playing with a boy named Ernie Ammons. We were in the same second-grade class at school, and this was our first chance to play together on our own. Ernie lived in town, and he had a new bicycle that he had just learned to ride. He was determined that I was going to learn to ride it also before that very day was over.

> The world stands on three pillars as its support: justice, truth, and peace. Justice requires truth-telling and results in peace. The three cannot be separated, or the world collapses. *(Sefer Ha-Aggadah* 733.128)

The yard at Ernie Ammons's house was a long side yard that sloped, not too steeply, down a long incline to Hospital Street. After convincing me that the secret of riding a bike was to get up enough speed to keep your balance, Ernie got me on the bicycle at the top of the yard. He held it upright while I got on the seat, then he started pushing it along until it was rolling down the yard on its own. Sure enough, when it got up enough speed, it kept its own balance!

I was riding! In the same instant I saw a car go past on Hospital Street and knew that I didn't know how to stop the bicycle. My feet weren't even on the pedals—it was just rolling.

"Help!" I heard myself scream. In the same instant my mother, who was visiting with Mrs. Ammons while I played with Ernie, saw the scene and screamed "Help!" too.

In what seemed like only a brief moment, the bicycle came to a gentle stop—just short of Hospital Street.

Mr. Ammons had heard both screams. He jumped up and ran, and caught the bicycle (with me on it), pulling it to a halt.

> Wisdom is the blessing offered to all the peoples of the world, not just to Israel. Such wisdom is creative of good things wherever it appears. When God wishes to punish those same nations, wisdom is taken away. Such lack of divine wisdom leads to destruction wherever it is lacking. *(Genesis Rabbah* 89.6)

I did not want to be killed; Ernie Ammons did not want me to be killed; my mother did not want me to be killed. But it was only the strength (not the will) of Mr. Ammons that could carry out our wish for the justice of caring for a foolish child. He was strong enough to be gentle. *(Donald Davis)*

Index of Readings from
The Revised Common Lectionary

187

Index of Midrashim

Ecclesiastes Rabbah

Song of Songs Rabbah

Sefer Ha-Aggadah